National Heritage Memorial Fund
Annual Report and Accounts for the year ended 31 March 2018

Report presented to Parliament pursuant to Section 7(1) of the National Heritage Act 1980, and accounts presented to Parliament pursuant to Section 7(3) of the National Heritage Act 1980

Ordered by the House of Commons to be printed on 11 July 2018
Laid before the Scottish Parliament by the Scottish Minister on 11 July 2018
Laid before the Northern Ireland Assembly on 13 July 2018
Laid before the National Assembly for Wales on 17 September 2018

HC 1315
SG/2018/94

Any enquiries related to this publication should be sent to us at
National Heritage Memorial Fund, 7 Holbein Place, London,
SW1W 8NR

This publication is available at https://www.gov.uk/government/
publications

ISBN 978-1-5286-0601-1

CCS0618945008   07/18

Printed on paper containing 75% recycled fibre content minimum.

Printed in the UK by the APS Group on behalf of
the Controller of Her Majesty's Stationery Office

Contents

Foreword by Sir Peter Luff
Chair of the National Heritage Memorial Fund

The NHMF plays an important role in helping to save for the public a rich variety of our nation's heritage, and its work deserves to be more widely known. Over thirty-eight years we have funded acquisitions ranging from notable landscapes and buildings, to documents and artefacts of great historical importance, from celebrated works of art to unusual objects of popular culture. In 2017–18, we have once again helped to secure the future of a varied and intriguing mix of heritage – from Hestercombe Garden's historic landscape to magnificent Viking treasures; from a Wedgwood vase to Marc Brunel's designs for the Thames Tunnel.

NHMF was set up in 1980 to save the best of our national heritage for the public, as a lasting memorial for those who lost their lives for the country in armed conflict. Today, and thanks to continued Government funding, we are proud of our role helping to save treasures that represent the best of the culture and society that so many thousands have died to protect. The continued commitment from the Government to fund the NHMF means that we can also help deliver the priorities of the Heritage Statement 2017, published by the Department for Digital, Culture, Media and Sport (DCMS) as the Government's vision for heritage and the historic environment.

The Fund works for people throughout the UK, ensuring the heritage of their area, region or country is saved and accessible to all. Wherever possible we like to help aspects of our heritage that have a distinct memorial character, so this year I was particularly pleased that we were able to help save two works by Eric Ravilious, who served as a war artist in the Second World War. Ravilious was declared lost in action in 1942 after the plane he was travelling in, on a mission off the coast of Iceland, failed to return. Both *Beachy Head* and *Two Women in a Garden*, will now remain in the collections at the Towner Art Gallery in Eastbourne and the Fry Art Gallery in Saffron Walden respectively.

"NHMF works for people throughout the UK, ensuring the heritage of their area is saved and accessible to all."

Ravilious was active in the 20th Century, but this year we were also able to save much earlier items. The stunningly beautiful East Cambridgeshire Bronze Age gold torc was one of several items declared Treasure that we helped to fund and which have been unearthed by metal detectorists across the UK.

The First World War precipitated the extension, in 1918, of the franchise to all men and to women over thirty. In this centenary year we were delighted to help Charleston in East Sussex to secure a set of dinner plates featuring forty-eight famous women from history. Painted by Duncan Bell and Vanessa Grant, part of the Bloomsbury group of writers and artists from the 1930s, the women illustrate the increased significance and understanding of female stories and histories in society at the time, and the growing emphasis on them.

Alongside the seventeen acquisitions we supported this year, we also concluded the Listed Places of Worship: Roof Repair Fund, operated by NHMF on behalf of DCMS. 907 places of worship were awarded a total of £53.4million through the scheme. I would like to thank all those NHMF staff who worked on the Roof Repair Fund over the past two years, for their hard work and exemplary dedication. This enabled important repairs to be made to places of worship to protect them for the communities they serve.

I also extend my thanks to all those who work at NHMF and to our advisory panel, our investment panel and our trustees, for their commitment to the UK's heritage. Our funds are limited and must be stewarded and spent wisely to have the maximum impact. This year their expertise and efforts have again helped to save some truly outstanding pieces from our nation's history – securing them for the benefit of future generations.

Sir Peter Luff
Chair of NHMF

> "This year (NHMF staff) expertise and efforts have again helped to save some outstanding pieces from our nation's history."

Famous Women Dinner Service

£310,000

The Famous Women Dinner Service was commissioned by Kenneth Clark in the 1930s from the Bloomsbury artists Vanessa Bell and Duncan Grant.

The 50 plates feature twelve queens, twelve women famed for their beauty, twelve writers and twelve performers, plus one plate depicting Bell and one depicting Grant. Each plate was designed and hand painted by the artists on commercially produced, blank plates made by Wedgwood.

The final 48 famous women make a particularly interesting list, representing often untold and suppressed female stories and histories. The plates feature Elizabeth Barrett Browning, the poet who

disobeyed her father to marry Robert Browning
and escape to Italy; Nell Gwyn, a long-time mistress
of King Charles II; and Catherine the Great, 18th
century Empress of Russia.

The collection was offered for sale to the Charleston
Trust, who run Charleston, the former home of
Bell and Grant. With support from NHMF, the
Trust was able to secure the sale and prevent the
collection from being broken up or sold abroad.

East Cambridgeshire Bronze Age Gold Torc Acquisition
Ely Museum
£150,000

A metal detectorist found this unique Bronze Age torc in a field in East Cambridgeshire. It is thought to be the largest found in England in more than a century and is of exceptionally fine quality.

As the torc is so large, there has been much speculation about what it might have been used for. It could have been worn over thick clothing; used to ornament a sacrificial animal or statue; or even worn by pregnant women as a form of protection. The torc sits alongside other recent discoveries from the fens, reflecting the importance and vibrancy of this area in the Bronze Age, with wide trade networks and skilled crafts people.

This extraordinarily rare and beautiful piece of history will now be on permanent display at Ely Museum, helping to tell the story of Bronze Age civilisation in and around the fens more than 3,000 years ago.

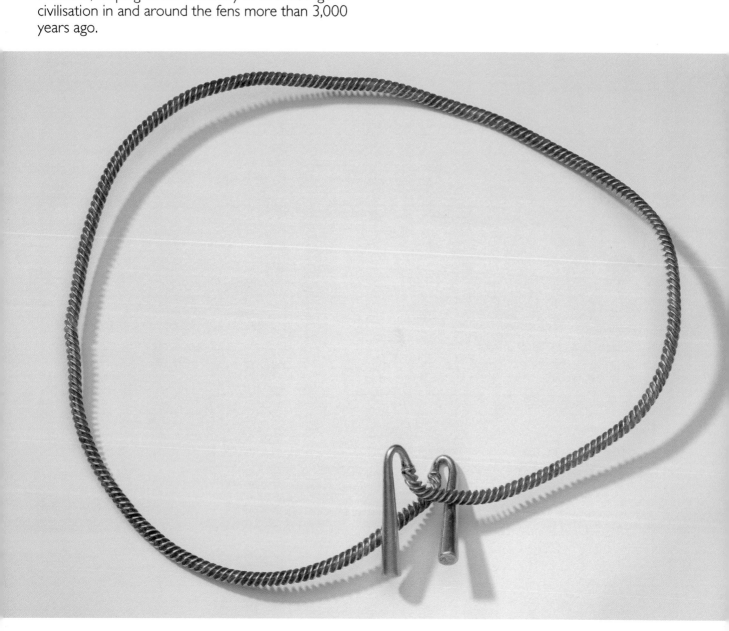

Saving *Queen Victoria*
Fitzwilliam Museum,
University of Cambridge

£267,607

This marble bust of *Queen Victoria* by Sir Alfred Gilbert was commissioned by the Army and Navy Club in 1887 to mark Queen Victoria's Golden Jubilee.

They commissioned Alfred Gilbert who was referred to as the 'leading British sculptor of his generation'. This bust is the finest example of Gilbert's work in marble, the majority of his pieces were cast in bronze; the best known is the 'Eros' Shaftesbury memorial in Piccadilly Circus, London.

The bust is a larger-than-life size, measuring 96cm tall, and shows the elderly Queen's features and expression in fascinating detail.

The sculpture had been provisionally sold to a museum in New York when the Secretary of State ruled that it was too closely associated with our national heritage and subjected it to an export licence deferral. During this time, the Fitzwilliam Museum was able to acquire the piece with the help of NHMF funding and save the sculpture for the nation.

Acquisition of the Clarke Collection: A Unique DH Lawrence Archive
University of Nottingham
£278,400

DH Lawrence (1885–1930) was one of the most important writers of the 20th century. His best-known works include *Sons and Lovers, Women in Love* and the controversial novel *Lady Chatterley's Lover*.

The Clarke collection, originally owned by Lawrence's sister Ada Clarke, is a unique and intimate record of Lawrence family life and their time in Nottinghamshire, which Lawrence drew on for his fictional world.

The collection includes a long series of letters and postcards from Lawrence to his sister Ada, from 1911 to just days before he died of tuberculosis in 1930. The correspondence reflects the writer's thoughts, work and relationships, throughout his travels across Europe, Asia, Australia, USA and Mexico.

The collection had been on long-term loan to the University of Nottingham since 1992 but without the support of NHMF funding, there was a risk the collection would be broken up and potentially sold abroad. The collection will now remain at the University of Nottingham in their DH Lawrence Collections.

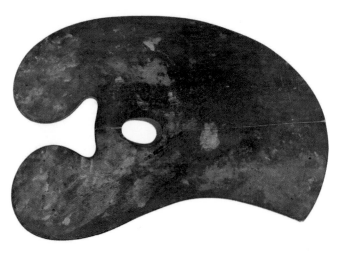

Top left: Sketch by Lawrence's elder brother of the two siblings together

Middle left: Draft poem My Love, My Mother (1911)

Bottom left: Artist's palette used by Lawrence at Santa Fe, New Mexico (c.1922–1925)

Above: Poncho believed to have been worn by Lawrence at Santa Fe, New Mexico (c.1922–1925)

Securing the future of *A Game of Bowls* at Ightham Mote
National Trust Ightham Mote

£175,000

Artist John Singer Sargent visited Ightham Mote in the late 1880s when the house was rented out to American railroad magnate and founder of Colorado Springs, William Jackson Palmer and his family. While he was visiting the house he produced sketches that were used in the painting of *A Game of Bowls*.

The people playing bowls are General Palmer's wife and daughter and their guests, including costume designer, Alice Comyns Carr; architect Fredrick Jameson and his wife; and Sargent's sister, Violet Sargent.

The painting captures a moment in the house's interesting history with a real-life scenario of the family hosting their artistic friends.

As a well-known portraitist, this is an unusual piece by Sargent and has been described as 'eccentric' in style. The painting was inherited by the Palmers' daughter Elsie and was more recently owned by American businessman A. Alfred Taubman and by Sotheby's auctioneers. It has more recently been on loan to the National Trust and Ightham Mote. Following the grant award from NHMF, the National Trust has been able to secure the painting for the future and will continue to exhibit it at Ightham Mote.

Acquisition of *Two Women in a Garden* by Eric Ravilious
Fry Art Gallery Society
£130,000

Two Women in a Garden is a rare early work by Eric Ravilious. The artist's well-known style was calm, muted in colour, geometric in precision and modernist, and his paintings rarely included people. Two Women is a striking contrast. It shows the beginnings of what was to become his distinctive style – geometric shapes, and a restrained palette – but its focus is the women.

The two women in the painting are the artist Tirzah Ravilious, the artist's wife; and Charlotte Bawden, also an artist, who was married to Edward Bawden. The couples had moved to Brick House, Great Bardfield, together in the 1930s. The watercolour dates from the time when Great Bardfield was becoming the focal point for a group of artists and designers later to be known as the Great Bardfield Artists. It has been interpreted either as a tribute to the idyll of country living or a more personal point about the domestic arrangements at Brick House.

Having been on loan to The Fry Art Gallery, in Saffron Walden, nearby to Great Bardfield, for a number of years, Eric Ravilious formed an immediate friendship with Edward Bawden and others from their student days at the Royal College of Art. Ravilious painted many scenes of Bardfield and Castle Hedingham, which they later moved to. An NHMF grant has enabled the Gallery to purchase the painting from the artist's family and the painting will now become part of the Gallery's permanent collection.

Top: The Mostyn Hours, The British Library, Additional 89250, ff.8v-9, calendar page for March with Aries and a labourer trimming vines

Right: The Mostyn Hours, The British Library, Additional 89250, ff.30v-31, the anointing of David, at the beginning of Psalm 26

Acquisition of the Mostyn Psalter Hours
The British Library

£390,000

This rare and beautiful manuscript is a combination of a Psalter (a volume of Psalms) and a book of hours (a volume of prayers to be said throughout the 'hours' of the day). It is one of just a few surviving examples of luxury books made in London in the late 13th century. The writing in the book includes highly decorative images and letters, and illustrations in the calendar of the labours of the months and the signs of the Zodiac.

The calendar features a sequence of London saints – including the seventh-century bishops of London, Melitus and Erkenwald – and the feast of the translation of Edward the Confessor in Westminster in 1269.

With the help of NHMF funding, the British Library has added the Psalter-Hours to its collection and the book has been digitised so that it is accessible for everyone to enjoy.

Anglo-Saxon Aristocrats from 'near Diss'

£90,900

Back in 2015, metal dectectorists discovered a 7th century grave near Winfarthing in South Norfolk. An archaeological excavation later recovered an outstanding range of items from gold jewellery, to a bowl, an iron knife and an iron buckle.

The grave goods are a group of high status items, which belonged to a wealthy 7th century Anglo-Saxon woman. These included an exquisite gold and garnet pendant, two coin-pendants of Merovingian King Sigeberht III, and a gold pendant cross. The decoration on the largest pendant bears close similarities with the jewellery found at nearby Sutton Hoo.

The goods together can help to build an understanding of the process of Anglo-Saxon society's conversion to Christianity and the custom of burial with grave goods. These finds reflect a woman who was Christian, buried with a cross, but not yet buried in a church or churchyard, still within Anglo-Saxon custom.

NHMF's grant to Norfolk Museums Service will now help the finds become a focal point of permanent displays at Norwich Castle Museum and Art Gallery.

Top: Large pendant excavated from the grave at Winfarthing

Bottom: First and fifth items: two coins struck by King Siegbert III (c.630-656)

Second and fourth items: conical 'spacer' beads

Middle item: cross-shaped pendant inlaid in gold filigree wire, indicating the buried women's Christianity

Paradise Restored: Reuniting Hestercombe's historic landscape
Hestercombe Gardens Trust

£1,485,000

Hestercombe gardens and landscape sit within an historic estate in Somerset, which was first mentioned in an Anglo-Saxon charter of 682.

The exceptional landscape reflects garden design over 400 hundred years, with a Georgian landscape garden, a Victorian terrace, and an Edwardian formal garden. The historic landscape is registered Grade 1 on the Historic England Register of Parks and Gardens.

The grant to Hestercombe Gardens Trust from the NHMF, will help to reunite the designed landscape. The acquisition includes almost the whole medieval park, a rare late 16th century watergarden, 18th century serpentine lakes and lost elements of Sir Edwin Lutyens' formal gardens.

Hestercombe Gardens Trust will now work to restore these landscapes and make them accessible to the public.

A selection of objects from the Galloway Hoard

Galloway Hoard
National Museums Scotland
£1,000,000

The Galloway Hoard is the richest collection of Viking-age objects ever found in Britain. It includes a number of silver items as well as gold objects, which are extremely rare in Viking finds.

The hoard had remained untouched for around 2,000 years after it was buried at the beginning of the 10th century in Dumfries and Galloway. A metal detectorist unearthed the collection in September 2014, helping to discover more than 100 objects. The hoard contained a range of precious metal and jewelled items, including a rare gold ingot, a unique gold bird-shaped pin and a decorative silver-gilt vessel. This vessel contained further unusual objects, such as beads, amulets of glass and rock crystal, and Anglo-Saxon disc brooches.

The collection was declared a Treasure Trove, with a value of £1,982,000 and offered to National Museums Scotland. They then had just six months to raise these funds and were able to achieve their target with the help of a £1,000,000 NHMF grant; funding from the Scottish Government, Art Fund and charitable trusts; as well as widespread public support.

National Museums Scotland will now carry out vital restoration works to the objects before they go on display to the public once again.

Monson Papers
Lincolnshire County Council
£242,500

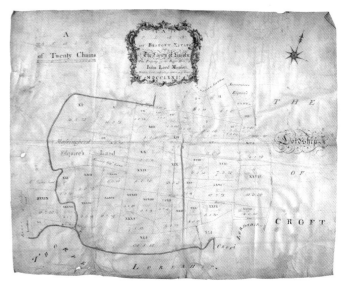

The Monson Collection contains important artworks, letters and travel papers spanning a 700-year period.

The collection is a major archive of the Monson family, which includes an invitation to the coronation of Queen Victoria and a contemporary copy of a report of Nelson's victory at the Battle of the Nile.

The archive also contains important records of domestic life, including receipts for furniture and family recipes. Together, these provide a fascinating insight into the everyday lives of people in the 18th and 19th century.

If the collection had not been purchased, there was a serious risk that the records would be withdrawn from the Lincolnshire Archives, where they had been on long-term loan since 1951. Thanks to an NHMF grant, this important piece of British history will now remain available to the public and be made accessible in new and exciting ways.

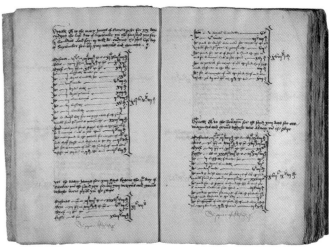

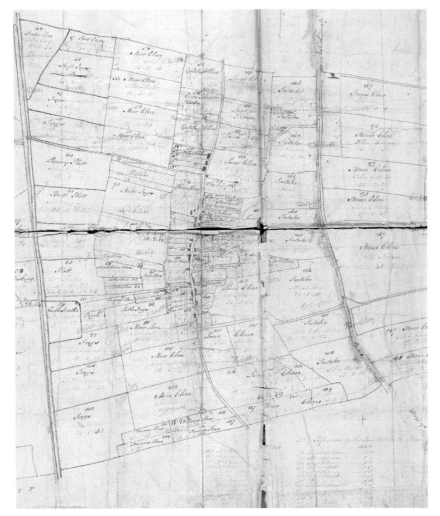

Top: plan of the estates of Lord Monson at Croft, near Wainfleet

Middle: Accounts of John Dawtry concerning the King's Warres (1513)

Left: Map of Saxby All Saints – late 18th century

Owen Jones – designs for Examples of Chinese Ornament
Victoria and Albert Museum
£112,500

Owen Jones was one of the most influential designers of the 19th century. An architect by profession, he designed the interiors and layout of the exhibits for the Great Exhibition of 1851.

In his design work, Jones searched for a more modern style to rival the neoclassical and Gothic Revival movements, by studying ornament outside of Europe. This convinced him that flat, abstract patterns and most importantly, colour, were the way forward.

The 51 original designs created for publication in *Examples of Chinese ornament selected from objects in the South Kensington Museum and other collections (1867)* show the development of his thinking about Chinese decoration. He sourced many of the designs from artefacts in the collections of the South Kensington Museum, which was later to become the Victoria and Albert Museum.

Having acquired the designs with the help of an NHMF grant, the V&A will now carry out extensive research to find source objects and compare the designs; and to trace the influence of Jones's Chinese patterns on the work of other designers.

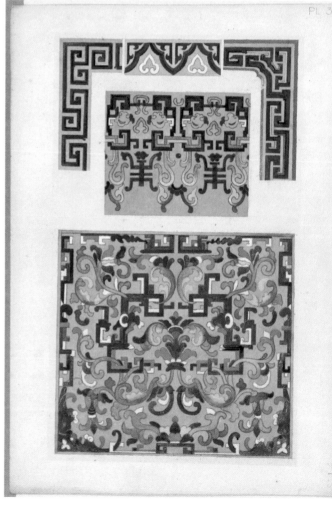

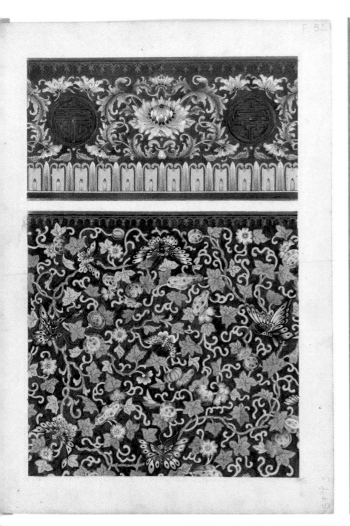

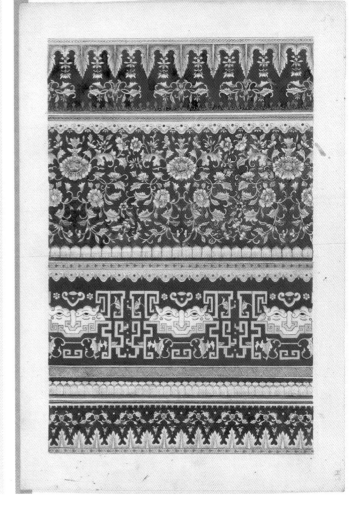

First Day's Vase
Potteries Museum & Art Gallery

£267,500

Wedgwood's First Day's Vase was made on the first day of production at the Wedgwood factory in Staffordshire in 1769. It was thrown by Josiah Wedgwood himself, with his business partner Thomas Bentley operating the wheel. Six vases were made on the first day, with just four surviving the firing process.

Wedgwood was one of the pioneers of the industrial revolution, with his factory at Etruria, being the first purpose-built pottery works in Staffordshire. The vases made on the first day of production were created in a neo-classical style, and painted with figures from Greek mythology – Oineus, Demophon and Chrysis. Each of the four vases has minor differences in decoration. This example is the only one to have 'egg and dart' on the rim of the vase

and base of the finial, making it unique. Wedgwood treasured these vases and dictated that they should never be sold.

Two of the other surviving vases are owned by the V&A Museum, while the third remains in the Wedgwood family. This fourth vase had been on loan to the Potteries Museum for over 30 years, when it was put up for auction. The museum attempted to secure it at the sale, with the aid of an NHMF grant. It was sold to an overseas collector and a temporary export bar was placed on the vase by the government. This gave the Potteries Museum enough time to, once more, raise the money needed to save it. Another NHMF grant joined funding from other grant bodies and donations from hundreds of members of the public and local businesses, to finally secure the vase. It will now continue to be displayed at the Potteries Museum & Art Gallery in Stoke-on-Trent.

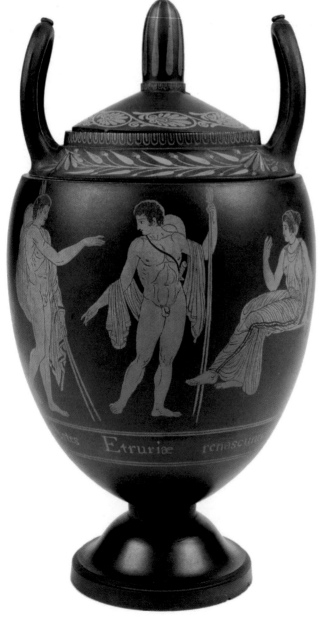

Eric Ravilious *Beachy Head*
Towner Art Gallery

£52,400

Eric Ravilious was one of the 20th century's most important artists. He was appointed an official war artist in World War II but was later killed while accompanying a Royal Air Force rescue mission off Iceland.

Beachy Head is considered one of Ravilious' most iconic works. It shows the hills and white chalk cliffs of Beachy Head outside Eastbourne – a world famous landmark; and depicts the area in the year of the outbreak of the Second World War. The landscape was changed shortly after by the barbed-wire and military defences used to secure the cliff from enemy invasion.

Towner Art Gallery's acquisition, with the help of NHMF funding, will now allow the artwork to be on regular display in Eastbourne where Ravilious lived in early childhood, regularly returning as an adult to paint and draw the South Downs. The painting is also being shown in touring exhibitions in Sheffield and Warwickshire during 2017 and 2018.

Tunnel Vision at The Brunel Museum
The Brunel Museum
£235,500

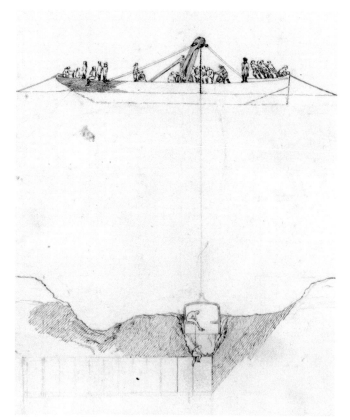

Sir Marc Brunel, father of Isambard Kingdom Brunel, was an acclaimed engineer. His most famous achievement was the Thames Tunnel – an engineering first – and now the oldest tunnel in the London Underground. Brunel's Tunnelling Boring Machine (TBM) has changed the shape of cities all over the world, and automated modern versions, such as Crossrail and the Channel Tunnel.

When the Tunnel opened in 1843, it was dubbed the Eighth Wonder of the World and people came from far and wide to see it.

The Thames Tunnel was the first tunnel under a river anywhere in the world. During building work, the Tunnel flooded five times, and in the worst flood, six men drowned and Isambard Kingdom Brunel barely escaped with his life.

The Brunel Museum is located directly above the Thames Tunnel in the Engine House and Grand Entrance Hall, the original entrance to the Tunnel. The entrance is now a museum gallery and performance space. NHMF provided a grant to acquire an album of drawings and watercolour designs for the Thames Tunnel as part of the Sir Marc Brunel Collection.

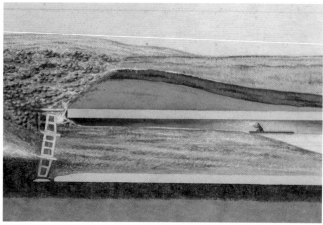

Top and middle: Drawings from Sir Marc's collection show a daring young Brunel first in a diving bell and then in a boat inside the tunnel inspecting the damage by lantern light

Below: Designs for the Thames Tunnel

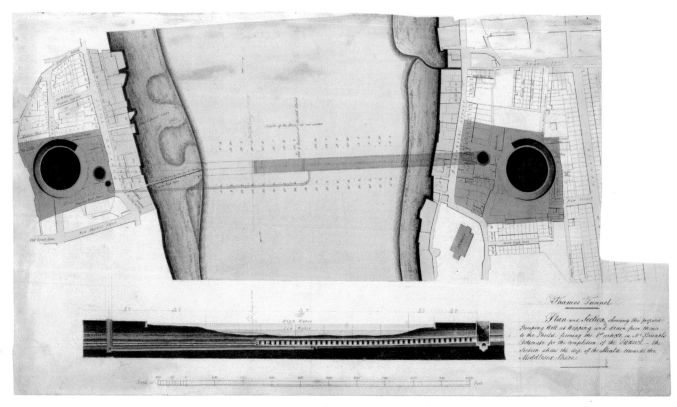

Sir Marc Brunel – collection for the Being Brunel Museum and Brunel Institute
SS Great Britain Trust

£160,202

After fleeing France at the time of the French Revolution, Sir Marc Brunel spent some time in the United States, before the requirements of the Royal Navy brought him to England. While living in the US, he was appointed Chief Engineer of the city of New York. He designed civic buildings, machines to dredge the river Mohawk and private houses, among other projects. The collection acquired by SS Great Britain Trust at auction includes plans for these projects, including those for public buildings that do not survive anywhere else. New York's official records were destroyed in a city-wide riot in 1863.

With the support of NHMF, the SS Great Britain Trust purchased the archive of 40 outstanding plans, diaries, drawings and photographs, including a watercolour design for Sir Marc's steam-powered sawmill at Chatham's Royal Naval Dockyard. This design, along with a selection of others, are now on display for the first time at the Being Brunel Museum which opened at the end of March 2018 alongside SS Great Britain in Bristol.

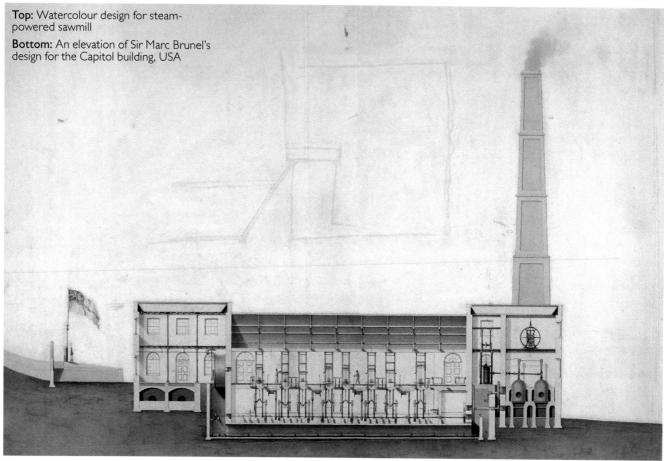

Top: Watercolour design for steam-powered sawmill

Bottom: An elevation of Sir Marc Brunel's design for the Capitol building, USA

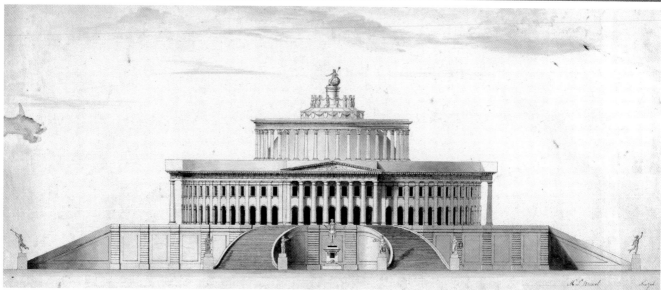

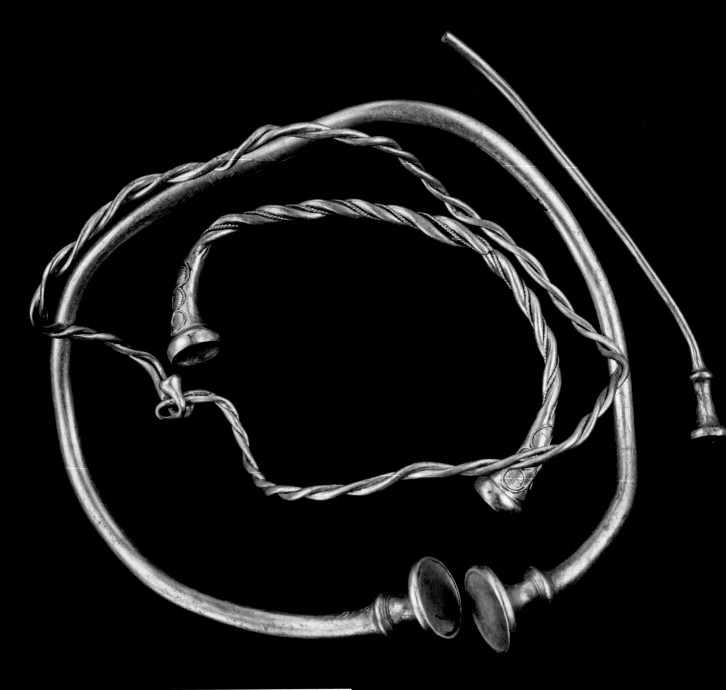

Leekfrith Torcs

£165,000

These four torcs – three necklaces and a bracelet – are believed to date back to around 400BC and were probably worn by important women in society.

They were discovered by metal detectorists in the Staffordshire Moorlands and may have originally come from the continent, possibly Germany or France. In particular, the bracelet has similarities with jewellery from the important Waldalgesheim hoard discovered in Germany in 1869.

It also represents some of the earliest Celtic art found in Britain. It is known as the 'Early Style' and is very rare on objects found in Britain. The bracelet, along with the other torcs will now be put on permanent display at Stoke-on-Trent's Potteries Museum and Art Gallery.

Report of the trustees and accounting officer

Performance report

Overview

Purpose – the purpose of the performance report is to provide information on the Board of Trustees, the organisation's main objectives and strategies and the principal risks it faces. The overview section gives the user information to understand the Board, its purpose, the key risks to the achievement of its objectives and how it has performed during the year. The analysis section is where the Board reports on its most important performance measures, including analysis using financial information from the financial statements.

Our performance in 2017–18:
A statement from the Chief Executive

2017–18 was a very busy and important year for the Heritage Lottery Fund (HLF) and National Heritage Memorial Fund (NHMF or the Fund). The work we undertook during this period has helped us to lay the foundations for the future. The fact that at the same time we successfully delivered the corporate priorities we set at the start of the year is a testament to the commitment of all the teams who work on the NHMF side of our business, the leadership of the Board of Trustees (the Board) and the strength of the Leadership Team.

We have concluded the Listed Places of Worship: Roof Repair Fund (LPOW Roof Repair Fund) work we started in 2014–15. On behalf of the government, over the last three years we have invested £53.4million into 907 places of worship across the UK in some exceptional and remarkable places including:

- Scarista Church, Isle of Harris, Scotland: built in 1840 in a remote location overlooking the Atlantic Ocean on the Outer Hebrides. A grant of £71,700 was awarded for repairs, and the level of partnership funding was particularly impressive considering the location and a small congregation of approximately 28, with over £30,000 being raised.

- Church of St Catherine, Temple, Cornwall: a Grade II* listed church on Bodmin Moor, which was founded by the Knights Templars in the12th century. It was later referred to as the 'Cornish Gretna Green' as marriage ceremonies were performed without a license until these became illegal in the 18th century. An LPOW Roof Repair Fund grant of £71,700 was awarded for repairs.

- The Church of St James in the Vale of Glamorgan, Wick, Wales: dates from the 12th century and was in need of urgent roof repairs to address 'nail sickness' and slate slippage, which led to water ingress and residual dampness in the church. A grant of £76,500 was awarded and the project again generated significant community interest and support.

- Cathedral Church of Christ the Redeemer, Dromore, Northern Ireland: dates from the 17th century and sits on a site used for Christian worship since 510AD when St Colman of Dromore established a small wattle and daub church. The Cathedral, which was dedicated by James I in 1609, was awarded £30,800 towards slate repairs.

The continuing work of the NHMF team on our standard grants has helped to save some remarkable items of heritage for the nation and widened public access to them.

The range of our grants in 2017–18 demonstrates the unique value that NHMF brings in supporting the nation's heritage, these included:

- East Cambridgeshire Bronze Age Gold Torc – Ely Museum

- Sir Marc Brunel Collection – SS Great Britain Trust

- Two Women in a Garden by Eric Ravilious – Fry Art Gallery

- Galloway Hoard – National Museums Scotland

- Owen Jones designs for Examples of Chinese Ornament – Victoria & Albert Museum

Building on the Spending Review settlement, we have used our annual grant-in-aid very effectively. With our endowment fund investments also performing well we took the opportunity to review our long-term investment strategy alongside the certainty of the Spending Review settlement to see what more we were potentially able to do. As a result, from April 2018, we have added an extra £750,000 a year to our £5million budget for NHMF.

The Tailored Review, which reported in November 2017, gave a strong positive endorsement of our NHMF work and we will continue to build on that in the future.

The development of a new Corporate Strategy will provide a roadmap for the Fund to seek further investment into the nation's heritage, for example through attracting and leveraging new investment opportunities to continue the impressive legacy we have built.

Finally, let me thank our NHMF staff. They work with great integrity and professionalism, are truly committed to the work of the Fund and provide an exceptional service to the nation's communities and heritage.

Report of the trustees and accounting officer

Our purpose and activities

NHMF is vested in and administered by, a body corporate known as the Trustees of the National Heritage Memorial Fund, consisting of a Chair and not more than 14 other members appointed by the Prime Minister. The Fund was set up on 1 April 1980 by the National Heritage Act 1980 ('the 1980 Act') in succession to the National Land Fund as a memorial to those who have given their lives for the UK. It receives an annual grant-in-aid from the government to allow it to make grants. The powers of the trustees and their responsibilities were extended by the provisions of the National Lottery etc. Act 1993 ('the 1993 Act'), the National Heritage Act 1997 ('the 1997 Act') and the National Lottery Act 1998.

Under the 1993 Act trustees also became responsible for the distribution of the proportion of National Lottery proceeds allocated to heritage. Trustees of NHMF have to prepare separate accounts for the receipt and allocation of grant-in-aid and for their operation as a distributor of National Lottery money. Trustees have chosen to refer to the funds as NHMF for sums allocated under the provisions of the 1980 Act and the Heritage Lottery Fund (HLF) for receipts under the provisions of the 1993 Act.

Under sections 3 and 3a of the 1980 Act, trustees may make grants and loans out of NHMF for the purpose of acquiring, maintaining or preserving:

i) any land, building or structure which in the opinion of the trustees is of outstanding scenic, historic, aesthetic, architectural, archaeological or scientific interest;

ii) any object which in their opinion is of outstanding historic, artistic or scientific interest;

iii) any collection or group of objects, being a collection or group which, taken as a whole, is in their opinion of outstanding historic, artistic or scientific interest.

Section 4 of the 1980 Act (as amended) extends the powers of trustees to improving the display of items of outstanding interest to the national heritage by providing financial assistance to construct, convert or improve any building in order to provide facilities designed to promote the public's enjoyment or advance the public's knowledge.

Under the 1980 Act (as amended) and the 1997 Act, trustees are now also able to assist projects directed to increasing public understanding and enjoyment of the heritage and to interpreting and recording important aspects of the nation's history, natural history and landscape. Trustees use these extended powers primarily in connection with HLF. Trustees believe that NHMF has a vital role as the central defence in protecting the nation's items of outstanding importance that are at risk. Trustees will continue to use the resources provided by government, as well as resources generated by its endowment fund, to offer financial assistance as a fund of last resort towards the acquisition, preservation and maintenance of heritage that is threatened by destruction or loss.

Our key issues and risks

Our key risk last year was the successful delivery of the remaining part of LPOW Roof Repair Fund and this was done in 2017–18 with all funds distributed to churches and other places of worship in line with the programme's objectives and outcomes.

We also managed the risk of the impact of Tailored Review recommendations on our operations.

Our ongoing risks remain the balance between demand for NHMF grants and the limited budget we have (£4.9million). We manage that by effectively prioritising grants, critically assessing requests and, where appropriate, directing these to our Lottery funding streams. Furthermore, we have agreed, given the advantageous position of the Endowment Fund, to direct some funds from there to the annual grant budget of up to £750,000 a year starting from 2018–19.

Finally, as we begin delivering our new Corporate Strategy, of which we provide more details of below, the set-up work for this area may need to be funded via our grant-in-aid, at least initially, until any new income streams became self-funding. We need to be alert to this and manage any financial risk prudently.

Going concern basis

The accounts have been prepared on a going concern basis. This is because assets significantly exceeded liabilities at the date of the statement of financial position and because trustees have set a grant award budget for 2018–19 that is not expected to alter that position. The Board has no reason to believe that the Fund will not continue to operate in the foreseeable future.

LPOW Roof Repair Fund has had a significant impact on our statement of financial position. This is simply the result of timing differences in that almost all our awards were made in 2014–15 and 2016–17, while the associated grant payments will be made in the years 2015–16 to 2018–19. We don't receive the grant-in-aid from the Department for Digital, Culture, Media and Sport (DCMS) until those grant payments are made, which means that the liability is recognised before we receive the grant–in-aid to clear them. Over time the impact of LPOW Roof Repair Fund will be neutral on our financial position.

Performance summary

The scale of our work means we have limited performance indicators but these are shown in the section of this report on key performance indicators on page 31. Our most significant indicator was as follows:

Indicator (for standard awards only)	Outcome in 2017–18
NHMF costs will be under 5% of grant-in-aid	Exceeded (2.8%)

We have met all our significant targets in 2017–18. No indicators have been set for the LPOW Roof Repair Fund programme other than the speed of grant payment.

Performance analysis

LPOW Roof Repair Fund was announced by the then Chancellor of the Exchequer ('the Chancellor') in the 2014 Autumn Statement. NHMF was asked by DCMS to run the programme aimed at listed places of worship, regardless of faith or denomination, throughout the UK. We received over 1,900 applications with a grant request of £105million by January 2015 and we made awards of £26.4million to over 500 places of worship in March 2015. A further £2million of grant increases was awarded in 2015–16. Most projects from this first tranche were successfully completed during 2016–17 with the remainder being finalised during 2017–18.

In response to the high demand, the Chancellor allocated a further £25million of funding for a second tranche of the programme to be committed during 2016–17. This was launched in late 2015 with an application deadline of February 2016. We received over 1,500 applications requesting £88million. Awards totalling £22.9million were made to over 400 applicants in June 2016. It was agreed with HM Treasury and DCMS that £1million of the £25million from 2016–17 could be carried forward to 2017–18 to provide funds for grant increases to those projects that had uncovered additional problems once repair work was underway. This amount was fully used during the year together with an additional £200,000 recycled from de-commitments from projects that did not require all their funding.

During 2017–18, over 160 projects from the second tranche of LPOW Roof Repair Fund were completed. The remainder are all underway and should be finalised by the end of June 2018. In addition to an external evaluation of the LPOW Roof Repair Fund programme, which was received in March 2017, LPOW Roof Repair Fund staff have been carrying out their own evaluation of the programme. The results of that work are being collated and will contribute to lessons learned to help inform the future work of NHMF.

Excluding LPOW Roof Repair Fund, the NHMF received 17 applications all of which were funded by trustees to the total of £5,512,109. This year, as in past years, NHMF has supported the acquisition of a wide range of important and significant heritage across the UK.

We were particularly pleased that the Potteries Museum and Art Gallery managed to acquire the First Day's Wedgwood vase. Last year the museum failed to secure the vase at auction. However the vase had an export deferral licence placed on it, which allowed the museum to re-apply to NHMF and successfully raise the requisite amount to secure the vase. Unusually, only one other acquisition came from items that were temporarily stopped from export. After a sale to the Metropolitan Museum of Art, New York, last year, a bust of *Queen Victoria* by Alfred Gilbert was the subject of an export licence deferral on the grounds that it met all three of the Waverley criteria. The Fitzwilliam Museum in Cambridge was successful in raising match funding and the bust will join their established collection of works by Gilbert and other artists from the New Sculpture movement.

This year saw the Memorial Fund support a range of significant archaeological items. The National Museums Scotland acquired the Galloway Hoard, which had been discovered in south west Scotland in 2014. It is the most important Viking-age hoard to be found in Scotland and is exceptional as an assemblage of rare items, including several that are unique finds for Viking-age Scotland. The museum displayed some of the hoard in late 2017 and intends to display items in both Edinburgh and Dumfries & Galloway. The Potteries Museum and Art Gallery acquired the Leekfrith torcs, which are thought to be early 3rd century, making them the earliest Celtic art form and earliest Iron Age gold torcs found in Britain. We supported two Treasure finds in the East of England. Ely Museum acquired the East Cambridgeshire Bronze Age gold torc dated to around 1300–1100BC. The torc is larger than any other Bronze Age torc found in England, and will become the focus of the museum's Prehistory Gallery and public engagement programme. Norfolk Museums and Archaeology Service acquired the finds from a 7th century Anglo-Saxon cemetery near Diss, which will form a central part of their Anglo-Saxon and Viking Gallery.

NHMF continues to provide funding to acquire or retain archives and literary heritage. We helped the British Library acquire the Mostyn Psalter-Hours, which is a rare example of a combined Psalter and Book of Hours dating back to the late 13th century. Lincolnshire Archives acquired the Monson Papers, a large collection comprising family and estate material spanning 500 years held on long-term

Report of the trustees and accounting officer

deposit by the Record Office. The collection shows how this Lincolnshire family played a major role in the life of the county through management of its estates, as well as local justice, military and political life. Nottingham University acquired the Clarke Collection of DH Lawrence material, which was owned by Lawrence's younger sister Ada. The collection had been on long-term deposit at the University and managed as part of their designated DH Lawrence collections.

Unusually, we supported two museums in the same auction to acquire archival material related to Sir Marc Brunel, which meant between them they acquired the majority of items for sale from the Brunel family collection. The Brunel Museum acquired an album of 30 watercolours and designs for the Thames Tunnel, compiled by Marc Brunel in 1834. The album includes work by Marc and Isambard Kingdom Brunel and other draughtsmen from the Brunel office. SS Great Britain Trust acquired material that includes designs for machinery, bridges and buildings, and also contains a manuscript biography of Marc Brunel by his daughter Sophia.

We also supported the acquisition of two watercolours by one artist, Eric Ravilious, although in this case it was by two separate museums. The Towner Art Gallery in Eastbourne acquired Ravilious' 1939 watercolour *Beachy Head*. This iconic view of the East Sussex coast is an excellent example of Ravilious' distinctive style of painting. It was part of the touring exhibition Ravilious and Co: The Pattern of Friendship. The Fry Art Gallery in Saffron Walden secured the watercolour, *Two Women in the Garden*, which depicts Charlotte Bawden and Tirzah Garwood, Ravilious' wife, in the garden of Brick House in Great Bardfield. Both connect to places influential to the artist in what was a relatively short career; the first the South Downs landscape, which he frequently painted and the latter the village where he was part of the artists' community of the 1930s and 40s.

Charleston in East Sussex is another place associated with a group of famous artists: the Bloomsbury Group. We supported the Charleston Trust to acquire the Famous Women Dinner Service made up of 50 plates. The service, commissioned in 1932 by Sir Kenneth Clark, was designed and hand painted by Vanessa Bell and Duncan Grant. There are four groups each comprising 12 plates depicting queens, beauties, writers and performers and two plates depicting Vanessa Bell and Duncan Grant. Bell and Grant painted the plates at Charleston and they will be displayed in Charleston's new exhibition gallery.

Ightham Mote, a National Trust property in the adjacent county of Kent, acquired *A Game of Bowls* by John Singer Sargent. Painted in 1889, the painting depicts a game of bowls taking place beside Ightham Mote, a Grade I listed house, which is one of the most complete small medieval manor houses in England. The work illustrates the importance of Anglo-American links in the extraordinary artistic community that congregated at Ightham in the 1880s.

The Victoria & Albert Museum acquired a set of 51 original designs by the 19th century architect and designer Owen Jones, which were painted for his book Examples of Chinese Ornament. The designs were recently rediscovered in a private collection in America. Chinese Ornament was published in 1867 and contained 100 chromolithographic plates of Chinese designs, some of which had been taken from objects in what was then the South Kensington Museum. The acquisition provides the museum with the opportunity to exhibit the paintings with the objects that influenced them, as well as taking rare original works by a highly important British designer into a national collection.

A significant acquisition by Hestercombe Gardens Trust of the freehold of almost the whole of the Hestercombe historic landscape means that the land will become publicly accessible and provide an integral experience of this historic landscape. The purchase of the land and Hestercombe Farm will reunite the designed landscape, securing almost the whole medieval park, a rare late 16th century water garden, 18th century serpentine lakes and lost elements of the Lutyens formal gardens. It is Grade I on the Historic England Register of Parks and Gardens and is an exceptional survival reflecting garden design over four hundred years.

A list of standard grants awarded is shown on page 29. Total standard grants awarded came to £5.7million. In addition, another £1.2million of LPOW Roof Repair Fund awards were made.

We received grant-in-aid of £12.458million in the year (2016–17: £35.3million). £5million was our standard annual grant and a further £7.458million was received towards our grant payments and administrative costs for running LPOW Roof Repair Fund. We had the few remaining unpaid LPOW Roof Repair Fund grant awards from 2014–15 and 2015–16, along with payments for a significant portion of the second tranche of awards made in 2016–17 and 2017–18. As a result of LPOW Roof Repair Fund activity declining, the reported operating deficit has declined markedly falling to £6.4million. LPOW Roof Repair Fund awards fell from £23.7million to £1.2million in 2017–18. These wild fluctuations in reported deficits should come to an end in 2018–19 as LPOW Roof Repair Fund finishes.

Also impacting upon the results for both 2016–17 and 2017–18 is a prior year adjustment. This has been created to reflect our belief that the level of

Acquisition	Applicant	Awarded
A Game of Bowls at Ightham Mote	National Trust	£175,000
Anglo-Saxon Aristocrats	Norfolk Museums Service	£90,900
Clarke Collection of DH Lawrence material	University of Nottingham	£278,400
East Cambridgeshire Bronze Age Gold Torc	Ely Museum	£150,000
Eric Ravilious *Beachy Head*	Towner Art Gallery	£52,400
Famous Women Dinner Service	Charleston Trust	£310,000
First Day's Vase	Potteries Museum and Art Gallery	£267,500
Galloway Hoard	National Museums Scotland	£1,000,000
Leekfrith torcs acquisition	Potteries Museum and Art Gallery	£165,000
Monson Papers	Lincolnshire County Council	£242,500
Mostyn Psalter Hours	The British Library	£390,000
Owen Jones – designs for 'Examples of Chinese Ornament'	Victoria & Albert Museum	£112,500
Paradise Restored: Reuniting Hestercombe's historic landscape	Hestercombe Gardens Trust	£1,485,000
Saving *Queen Victoria*	Fitzwilliam Museum	£267,607
Sir Marc Brunel – collection for the Being Brunel Museum and Brunel Institute	SS Great Britain Trust	£160,202
Tunnel Vision at The Brunel Museum	The Brunel Museum	£235,500
Two Women in a Garden by Eric Ravilious	Fry Art Gallery Society	£130,000
Total standard grants awarded		**£5,512,509**

LPOW Roof Repair Fund liabilities was significantly overstated at 31 March 2017. It is the nature of repair projects, especially to historic buildings where the roofs may not have been fully inspected for years, that the full extent of damage is not known until the work begins. This meant that project costs included in grant applications were sometimes optimistic and sometimes pessimistic. In the case of the former, we have been able to give grant increases; in the latter we have to make de-commitments. Our process for recognising de-commitments appears to have been unduly prudent in that we continued to recognise as liabilities sums that are highly unlikely to be claimed. The adjustment therefore reduces by over £924,000 our liabilities at the end of March 2017.

Despite the reported operating deficit we had almost £46million of net assets at the year end, although £16million of this relates to the unrealised surplus in the value of the endowment fund. In addition, trustees have received an allocation letter from DCMS that makes it clear that NHMF will receive sufficient grant-in-aid in the next few years to cover its liabilities and planned grant budgets.

In addition to its impact on our level of awards, LPOW Roof Repair Fund continues to distort our administrative costs. The level of LPOW Roof Repair Fund costs fell significantly as the programme wound down to its expected conclusion in June 2018. Most LPOW Roof Repair Fund staff moved back to HLF work resulting in a large reduction in both staff and other administrative costs.

In addition to continuing our work on the LPOW Roof Repair Fund programme, we also accepted donations from Tourism NI and the Department for Communities towards the costs of some of the awards we made in Northern Ireland in 2017–18. Our contribution towards these grants was made using Lottery money and are disclosed in our National Lottery distribution accounts, but the awards made on behalf of Tourism NI and the Department for Communities are disclosed in these accounts. Readers of our new Corporate Strategy will see that we hope to undertake more of these agreements in the future.

The return on the endowment in the year was a rise of 1.1%. The rate of return was well down on the 17.5% of last year. Obviously, whilst our investment managers apply their expertise, the main influence on return is the performance of world stock markets, which had a dip in the latter part of the year. The endowment fund investment policy remained one of capital accumulation, but the trustees' Investment Panel has updated the strategy and part of the fund will be switched from capital accumulation to income generation in 2018–19.

Cash figures rose during the year to £7million. We have well over £5million of grant liabilities. We drew down all the remaining LPOW Roof Repair Fund funding from DCMS in case there was a late surge of grant payments towards the year end – this proved not to be the case.

Report of the trustees and accounting officer

Key performance indicators by year

	Target	2017–18	2016–17	2015–16	2014–15	2013–14	2012–13
Application processing times (months)							
— urgent applications	3	**1.2**	1.0	0.9	0.7	1.3	1.2
— non-urgent applications	6	**2.3**	4.7	0.9	1.4	2.2	2.6
Publicising decisions (working days)							
— post decisions on website	14	**20**	20	20	10	10	10
Grant payment (number of working days after payment request)							
— Standard grants	15	**8**	2	4	3	5	4
— LPOW Roof Repair Fund	10	**4**	5	2	n/a	n/a	n/a

A change in our system of uploading decisions on our website in 2015–16 meant that we could no longer meet the target set for us in our management agreement with DCMS.

The above indicators and targets will continue into 2018–19.

Outstanding grant liabilities fell from £7.9million (after the prior year adjustment) to £5.3million. The decline is mostly due to us only making net awards of around £926,000 to the LPOW Roof Repair Fund in the year whilst paying out over £6million. When LPOW Roof Repair Fund finishes in 2018–19, our grant liabilities will settle back to the long-term trend.

Key performance indicators
Trustees recognise that NHMF should strive for high performance in its activities. To this end there are three performance indicators in our current funding agreement with DCMS (along with the administrative efficiency indicator reported above). These indicators cover the most significant aspects of customer service – the speed of processing a grant application; the speed of processing a grant payment request; and the speed of publicising decisions on our website. The Fund is achieving the majority of its targets thereby demonstrating an effective service to our applicants and grantees.

Payables
NHMF adheres to the government-wide standard on bill-paying and the Public Contracts Regulations 2015, which states that all valid bills should be settled within 30 days. In 2017–18 the average age of invoices paid was five working days (2016–17: five working days). Over 96% of invoices were paid within 30 calendar days (2016–17: 95%).

Another way of measuring our commitment to paying suppliers is the ratio of creditor days – the ratio of trade payables at the end of the year to the total value of purchases in the year expressed in terms of calendar days. At 31 March 2018, the figure was 30 days (2016–17: 29 days). The figure is much higher at the year-end than at other times of the year because we encourage suppliers to submit their invoices before the year ends.

Environmental policies and sustainability reporting
HM Treasury requires all public sector bodies to produce an annual sustainability report. The compilation of this data is unfortunately not an exact science. For example, very few of the landlords of our 10 regional and country offices are prepared to provide us with figures for kilowatt hours of gas or electricity used nor are they able to bill quickly enough after a year-end to provide figures in time for the production of year-end accounts. As the majority of our offices are small occupancies with private sector landlords, fully robust reporting is a challenge. This means that we have to use estimates for most offices. In addition, we have signed a fixed cost contract with the supplier of water to our head office, which means we no longer receive consumption data. The overall position is improving slightly over time but we still have to estimate much of our consumption. From 2013–14 we also started to calculate our carbon dioxide equivalent consumption for water and waste.

Furthermore, the second table (on page 31) reports data on a full-time equivalent basis (FTE), i.e. the level of consumption per member of staff. However, as we also include emissions incurred by non-members of staff, e.g. trustees, committee members and certain suppliers, the comparability of some of these numbers, over the years and with other organisations, is difficult to support.

Finally, the conversion factors used to calculate the carbon dioxide equivalent of our emissions often vary year on year. Normally the changes are relatively small but, for example, the figures for certain refrigerants used in air conditioning rose by around 20% for 2016–17 while others fell.

Trustees see little point in allocating sustainability reporting between their grant-in-aid activities and their Lottery distribution activities. Consequently the information below covers the whole activities of NHMF.

Summary of performance

Our greenhouse gas emissions have fallen slightly in 2017–18 on a gross basis and also when looking at the numbers on an FTE basis.

NHMF has control over only one of the properties that it occupies, which is its headquarters at Holbein Place in London. In 2010–11 we replaced the chillers for the air conditioning and the 25-year-old gas boilers for the heating and installed sensor-controlled lighting that is both movement- and daylight-sensitive. Having undertaken such a major refit there is very little scope for further reducing greenhouse emissions in the one office we control. Specifically we would not consider any significant expenditure for long-term benefits until we had renewed our lease at Holbein Place. A rent review is due in 2019.

In the 10 other properties we occupy we are wholly reliant on the landlord to improve performance and that is unlikely to happen between major refurbishments. Our room for further improvement in scope one and two emissions is therefore extremely limited. Over the years we have relocated some of our regional and country offices into smaller premises or serviced offices, which will have reduced consumption. Since May 2011, we have also rented out part of one floor of Holbein Place with the effect of reducing the consumption that we report; although in 2016–17 the space rented out was reduced.

We also expect to reduce the size of future office leases with staff being encouraged to hot-desk and work more flexibly.

Greenhouse gas emissions

Direct energy emissions relate to gas used in boilers operated by NHMF and emissions given off through our use of air conditioning in our London headquarters. Information about gas consumption in kilowatt hours is derived from our suppliers' invoices. Kilowatt hours are converted to carbon dioxide equivalent tonnes using a conversion factor derived from the tables *UK Government GHG Conversion Factors for Company Reporting*. These tables are available at www.gov.uk/government/collections/government-conversion-factors-for-companyreporting.

Indirect energy emissions relate to electricity generated by other organisations and sold directly to us as well as heating that we buy from landlords of our country and regional offices. Information about consumption in kilowatt hours is obtained from our landlords where possible, although their methodologies can vary. Kilowatt hours are converted to carbon dioxide equivalent tonnes using the relevant conversion factor. We are heavily reliant on our landlords to improve efficiency.

Most of our travel is by rail and our main ticket supplier provides us with details of the carbon dioxide equivalent emissions for all journeys

Sustainability reporting

Area	2017–18	2016–17	2015–16	2014–15	2013–14	2012–13
Greenhouse gas emissions – scopes 1, 2 & 3 which incorporates business travel including international air and rail (tonnes CO$_2$ equivalent)	410	417	635	591	489	550
Estate energy – Consumption (mkWh)	0.9	0.7	1.1	1.1	0.9	1.1
– Expenditure (£)	437,986	488,315	488,361	429,425	445,624	489,638
Estate waste – Amount (tonnes)	26	23	28	26	28	24
– Expenditure (£)	25,908	19,115	13,268	14,095	12,400	5,518
Estate water – Consumption (m^3)	3,927	4,040	4,350	4,889	5,655	3,757
– Expenditure (£)	10,703	12,089	7,413	11,825	14,182	11,253

Sustainability reporting normalised by average FTE staff employed in the period

Area per FTE	2017–18	2016–17	2015–16	2014–15	2013–14	2012–13
Greenhouse-gas emissions – scopes 1, 2 & 3 which incorporates business travel including international air and rail (tonnes CO$_2$ equivalent)	1.4	1.4	2.3	2.3	1.9	2.2
Estate energy – Consumption (kWh)	2,899	2,524	4,105	4,134	3,595	4,249
– Expenditure (£)	1,470	1,648	1,744	1,639	1,716	1,986
Estate waste – Amount (tonnes)	0.1	0.1	0.1	0.1	0.1	0.1
– Expenditure (£)	87	65	47	54	48	22
Estate water – Consumption (m^3)	13	13	16	19	22	15
– Expenditure (£)	36	41	26	45	55	46

Report of the trustees and accounting officer

undertaken. Similarly, our main car hire supplier provides us with data on these emissions. Staff are required to update department spreadsheets with information about all other journeys undertaken by staff, trustees, committee members, expert panellists and suppliers on our register of support services (in effect the monitors and mentors that we appoint to oversee projects that we are co-funding). Department heads are tasked to ensure that their staff record all their travel. The information gathered is converted to tonnes of carbon dioxide equivalent using the relevant parts of the same tables of conversion factors.

Waste

Waste generation has risen slightly in 2017–18 mainly as a result of the relocating of two offices – Cambridge and Manchester – as well as the closure of our main offsite storage base as part of a digitisation project. It is inevitable that the level of waste increases when an office move occurs as the opportunity is taken to dispose of surplus items accumulated over the years.

However, we have to be careful about the accuracy of the overall numbers because, as discussed below, there is no reliable measure of the amount of waste we generate, as it is simply taken away by councils, and it would not be an appropriate use of resources to procure weighing equipment simply for the purpose of improving our reporting of this figure. We will continue to seek a practical solution to calculating a reliable figure. We believe that the 2015–16 figure was higher than the long-term trend as it was impacted by significant office moves.

NHMF does not generate any hazardous waste. Further analysis of what happened to the waste we generated is not possible. All non-recycled waste is collected by councils local to the offices in which we operate. We do not know what they do with that waste and have made assumptions as to where the waste goes in order to produce the figures on page 31. Only the Royal Borough of Kensington & Chelsea invoices us separately, but we also include the cost of securely removing shredded paper into the figures. We strive to reduce the amount of paper that we use and then, inevitably, throw away and the photocopying budget for 2018–19 has been significantly cut. Greater sanction is being placed on teams should they exceed their photocopying budget, electronic devices are being distributed to staff to encourage them to have paper-free meetings and we recognise that new offices will have to be smaller than existing ones when leases expire.

We also aim to digitise most of our archive storage during the coming year. This will inevitably lead to a one-off increase in the amount of paper that we dispose of. However, the long-term cost savings should be substantial.

Our country and regional offices are small enough to weigh the waste they generate. There is no reliable way to measure the much greater volume of waste removed by the Royal Borough of Kensington & Chelsea because the council does not tell us the weight of what they remove. We have therefore estimated the amount of waste generated per person based on an estimate of the weight of a standard sack of waste.

Use of resources

Water consumption fell slightly in 2017–18. Where possible we persuade our landlords to provide information about the number of cubic metres of water consumed, which is normally based on the space we occupy rather than by individual metering. In 2015–16 we installed more efficient toilet facilities at our head office. We have also signed a fixed price contract for water supply for our head office. This has resulted in a much-reduced charge, but at the expense of the supplier not providing us with details of actual consumption. Consequently we have used the 2014–15 figure for analysis purposes.

Two years ago we undertook a review of electricity consumption at our head office. This involved an investigation of power usage on each floor through the placement of meters and by undertaking enhanced maintenance to improve the efficiency of our electrical devices. Estate energy consumption has fallen since then. We signed contracts to cap gas and electricity costs for our head office for 2016–17 and beyond. However, we have to accept that the weather has a bigger influence over our consumption than any improvements we can make to our energy efficiency.

Ros Kerslake OBE
Chief Executive and Accounting Officer
29 June 2018

Accountability report

Corporate governance report

The purpose of this corporate governance report is to explain the composition and organisation of NHMF's governance structures and how they support the achievement of our objectives.

The directors' report
Chair and trustees of NHMF

Chair
Sir Peter Luff [2]

Trustees
Baroness Kay Andrews OBE

Anna Carragher

Sir Neil Cossons OBE [1]

Sandie Dawe CBE
to 14 August 2017

Dr Angela Dean [1]

Jim Dixon

Dr Claire Feehily [1]
from 1 March 2018

Perdita Hunt DL, OBE [2]

Steve Miller

Richard Morris OBE

René Olivieri [2]
from 1 March 2018

Atul Patel MBE [2]

Dame Seona Reid DBE

Dr Tom Tew

Chief Executive
Ros Kerslake OBE [2]
from 4 July 2016

1 Member of Audit and Risk Committee
2 Member of Finance, Staffing and Resources Committee
   (which also covers remuneration)

Details of other senior managers can be found in the remuneration and staff report starting on page 42.

The gender split of our staff (including those on fixed term contracts) working on exchequer-related activities and our trustees at 31 March 2018 on a headcount basis was as follows:

	Male	Female	Total
Trustees	7	7	14
Directors	0	0	0
Staff	0	4	4

While we disclose four staff above, all the directors and staff in the support departments get involved in both our National Lottery distribution and grant-in-aid distribution activities. However, as the overwhelming majority of their time is spent on National Lottery distribution activities, their statistics are incorporated in those accounts.

Register of Trustees' Interests

As a matter of policy and procedure, the trustees declare any direct interests in grant applications and commercial relationships with NHMF and exclude themselves from the relevant grant appraisal, discussion and decision processes within NHMF.

In their contacts with grant applicants, trustees seek to avoid levels of involvement or influence that would be incompatible with their responsibilities as a trustee of NHMF. There are corresponding arrangements for staff to report interests and avoid possible conflicts of interest. The Register of Trustees' Interests is available on the HLF website – www.hlf.org.uk.

Future developments

In 2017–18 we created a Corporate Strategy, setting out our vision for the future role of NHMF over the three years from 2018 until 2021. We expect to undertake this work using our HLF brand although we anticipate that it will also involve funds from sources other than the National Lottery.

The National Lottery will remain our most significant source of income from 2018–2021, and the focus of most of our activity. The Corporate Strategy reinforces the direction we have been taking for several years, setting out our role as the largest dedicated source of funding for heritage across the UK, and taking further steps towards a stronger leadership position, with a particular focus on opportunities beyond pure grant giving.

Our Tailored Review recommendations support our ambitions to:

- take a stronger leadership position, setting clearer strategic priorities for heritage across the four countries of the UK within a UK-wide framework;

- develop commercial, financial, digital and inclusion skills in the heritage sector;

- test alternatives to pure grants, such as social investment and other types of repayable finance to increase the sustainability of the sector;

- support the sector in working internationally;

- fund and champion high quality digital projects;

- support the development of the National Lottery brand.

These recommendations provide the context for our Corporate Strategy and next Strategic Funding Framework for our National Lottery distribution activities.

Since 1994, our role in distributing National Lottery money has been to make 'a lasting difference for heritage and people in the UK'. We have developed a position as a heritage leader, through our influence and money, and significant capabilities, expertise and processes supporting grant distribution. In future we want to further recognise the wide-ranging benefits delivered for society through heritage and a broader role for NHMF as an enabler, both in leveraging investment for heritage from others and in developing capacity, skills and resilience in organisations and people.

Our vision is that by 2021, NHMF will be a strong strategic and thought leader for the full breadth of heritage across the UK, demonstrating and championing the impact and benefits to society that heritage achieves and leveraging investment and support from others to strengthen this position. Heritage will be more widely recognised as a vital contributor to GDP, social cohesion, better places and individual well-being.

We will deploy National Lottery income as grants, loans or other financial interventions where they will create most long-term value for society. We will maximise impact through recycling income and taking a share of increased income where appropriate, as well as leveraging non-Lottery investment in heritage from others.

We will be a collaborative investor, developing strategic relationships at scale, for example in place-making. We will champion innovation in business models, and build capacity, skills and resilience in organisations in heritage to enable them to diversify their income and attract new investment. We will use our expertise; and access to information, data and research; as an enabling leader and support the heritage world to better measure and demonstrate its social impact.

We will enhance our reputation as a highly efficient and effective administrator of National Lottery and Memorial Fund grants and seek to generate more income for NHMF in order to strengthen our business model and deliver benefits for UK heritage.

We can describe this change as moving from:
- simply distributing money raised by the National Lottery or the tax-payer to make a lasting difference for heritage and people in UK;

To:
- inspiring, leading and resourcing the UK's heritage to create positive and lasting change for people and communities, now and in the future.

Our Corporate Strategy was published in spring 2018. Find out more about our Corporate Strategy and Business Transformation Programme on pages 38 and 39.

Our standard grant-in-aid will be £5million for 2018–19 and the same amount for the final year of the current Spending Review. Our standard grant-in-aid (as opposed to additional sums provided to fund LPOW Roof Repair Fund) has remained at £5million for many years. Trustees recognise that

inflation lessens the impact of this sum. To this end, we have altered our investment strategy for the endowment fund. In recent years, capital accumulation has been the priority as trustees sought to return the value of the endowment to its target value, but now income generation has come more to the fore and trustees hope to add around £750,000 to the budget from 2018–19 onwards.

The LPOW Roof Repair Fund team has been reduced in size over the course of 2017–18 as projects have completed. Staff have been redeployed to other posts within NHMF, mainly on National Lottery distribution activities. The programme was completed in June 2018 so there was some residual work in 2018–19.

Appointment of auditors
The 1980 Act provides for the annual accounts of NHMF to be audited by the Comptroller and Auditor General. The 1993 Act extends this to the Lottery distribution activities of trustees.

Key stakeholders
The key stakeholder of NHMF is DCMS. We are also mindful of the needs of the heritage sector and the population of the UK when making decisions on applications for funding.

Personal data
NHMF has had no incidents where personal data was inadvertently disclosed to a third party and as such made no report to the information commissioner's office. NHMF will continue to monitor and assess its information risks in order to identify and address any weaknesses and ensure continuous improvement of its systems.

Statement of trustees' and accounting officer's responsibilities
Under section 7(3) of the 1980 Act, trustees of NHMF are required to prepare a statement of accounts for each financial year in the form and on the basis determined by the Secretary of State for the Department for Digital, Culture, Media and Sport with the consent of HM Treasury. The accounts are prepared on an accruals' basis and must give a true and fair view of the Fund's state of affairs at the year end and of its income and expenditure, recognised gains and losses and cash flows for the financial year.

In preparing the accounts, trustees of NHMF are required to comply with the government financial reporting manual (FREM) and in particular to:

i) observe the accounts' direction issued by the Secretary of State for Digital, Culture, Media and Sport, including the relevant accounting and disclosure requirements, and apply suitable accounting policies on a consistent basis;

ii) make judgements and estimates on a reasonable basis;

iii) state whether applicable accounting standards, as set out in the FREM, have been followed and disclose and explain any material departures in the financial statements; and

iv) prepare the financial statements on the going concern basis, unless it is inappropriate to presume that the Fund will continue in operation.

The principal accounting officer of DCMS appointed the senior full-time official, the Chief Executive, as Accounting Officer for the Fund. Her relevant responsibilities as Accounting Officer, including her responsibility for the propriety and regularity of the public finances for which the Accounting Officer is answerable, for the safeguarding of the Fund's assets and for the keeping of proper records, are set out in the section titled 'Accounting Officers' in *Managing Public Money*.

So far as the Accounting Officer is aware there is no relevant audit information of which our auditors are unaware. The Accounting Officer has taken all steps that she ought to have taken to make herself aware of any relevant audit information and to establish that our auditors are aware of that information.

The accounting officer confirms that the annual report and accounts as a whole is fair, balanced and understandable and that she takes personal responsibility for the annual report and accounts and the judgments required for determining that it is fair, balanced and reasonable.

Governance statement

Foreword

I have been Chief Executive and Accounting Officer since 4 July 2016. We have made a number of changes in our governance and internal controls in 2017–18, which are set out here. I am satisfied that there was a robust and proper control framework in place that allowed the system of internal controls to operate effectively during the period under review.

Introduction

This governance statement is a summary of the arrangements for the stewardship of the NHMF, including how we manage risk and how we comply with the 2017 HMT Corporate Governance in Central Government Departments: Code of Good Practice.

As the Accounting Officer for the National Heritage Memorial Fund, I am required by the Accounts Direction issued by the Secretary of State for Digital, Culture, Media and Sport to account separately for our two main sources of income – grant-in-aid and funds derived from the National Lottery. I am also accountable for maintaining a sound system of internal control that supports the achievement of NHMF's policies, aims and objectives, whilst safeguarding the public funds and assets for which I am personally responsible. This is

in accordance with the responsibilities assigned to me in *Managing Public Money*.

NHMF and HLF are operated as a single entity as I believe that this is more efficient and effective. Consequently, there is one governance structure and this statement covers the distribution of both grant-in-aid and National Lottery grants.

Governance structure

The governance structure of NHMF is set out in the diagram below.

Board of Trustees

The Board of Trustees is responsible for:

- Giving strategic leadership and direction;
- Approving control mechanisms to safeguard public resources;
- Approving grant programme and administration budgets;
- Supervising the overall management of NHMF activities and,
- Reporting on the stewardship of public funds.

The Board operates as a group and held nine meetings during the year to set NHMF policy and make decisions in line with that policy. These meetings are attended by the Chief Executive and the Senior Leadership Team. All Board meetings held in 2017–18 were quorate. Sir Peter Luff is Chair of the NHMF and throughout the year regular liaison meetings were held between the Chair, the Chief Executive and senior staff.

The Board is normally constituted of around 15 trustees including the Chair – this is the maximum permitted. In 2016–17 the number of trustees reduced to 13, this has increased to 14 in 2017–18 following a recent recruitment round in anticipation of several trustees retiring in the spring and summer of 2018. These changes were approved by our sponsor department – the DCMS and the Prime Minister (as trustee appointments fall within the remit of the Prime Minister).

The overall attendance rate of trustees at Board meetings was 91%. Trustees have also delegated some of their tasks to the two committees shown above – these committees oversee the activities of management and provide guidance and support to senior staff. The minutes of committee meetings are standing items at the Board's meetings. The Committee Chairs also provide a full report on their Board activities.

Report of the trustees and accounting officer

Attendance at Board meetings throughout 2017–18 was as follows:

Trustee	Eligible meetings	Meetings attended
Baroness Kay Andrews OBE	9	7
Anna Carragher	9	8
Sir Neil Cossons OBE	9	8
Sandie Dawe CBE to 14 August 2017	3	3
Dr Angela Dean	9	9
Jim Dixon	9	7
Dr Claire Feehily from 1 March 2018	1	0
Perdita Hunt DL, OBE	9	9
Sir Peter Luff	9	9
Steve Miller	9	9
Richard Morris OBE	9	7
René Olivieri from 1 March 2018	1	1
Atul Patel MBE	9	9
Dame Seona Reid DBE	9	8
Dr Tom Tew	9	9

Board composition
Of the 15 trustees who attended the Board throughout the year, 46% were female and 54% were male. One (8%) came from an ethnic minority group.

Board conflicts of interest
At the beginning of each Board meeting, all trustees and staff are asked to declare any potential conflict of interests. These are noted in the minutes, and trustees and staff remove themselves from Board discussions on those matters. Trustees and staff are also responsible for ensuring that entries in the Register of Interests are maintained and updated as necessary.

Audit and Risk Committee
The Committee met on four occasions during the year and was quorate at each meeting. It is chaired by a trustee.

The Chief Executive attended each Committee meeting with the Director of Finance and Corporate Services – other senior staff attended as required. The Committee is supported and serviced by the Fund's Secretariat. The Fund's external auditors (National Audit Office) and internal auditors (Moore Stephens) also attend the meeting. The Committee holds in-camera sessions themselves before meetings and also private discussions with the auditors before the meetings.

In 2017–18 the trustees decided to appoint non-executive independent members to supplement the trustees on the Committee. As a result, David Michael and Carole Murray joined the Committee in 2017. Both have considerable experience on risk management, governance and audit. The Terms of Reference for the Committee were updated to reflect their roles.

The Committee agreed a multi-year internal audit strategy with Moore Stephens upon their appointment and the reviews carried out in 2017–18 and reported to the Committee were in line with that strategic approach. A detailed one-year plan of internal audit reviews is approved annually.

During the year, the Committee received reports on:

- brand acknowledgement;
- health and Safety;
- IT project management,
- applications and project monitoring;
- core financial controls; and
- project post completion monitoring.

The Committee meeting minutes are shared with the Board as is a formal annual report on business. The Committee Chair orally updates the Board on Committee business and decisions.

The Committee also reviews the Annual Reports and Accounts for both NHMF and HLF. During 2017–18, in addition to the above reports and accounts, the Committee considered the following:

- the arrangements for continuing the new risk management processes at departmental level;
- fraud and alleged fraud cases; and
- procurement arrangements including any exceptions to normal procurement tendering rules.

Attendance at Committee meetings throughout 2017–18 was as follows:

Trustee	Eligible meetings	Meetings attended
Dr Angela Dean Chair	4	4
Sir Neil Cossons OBE from 1 September 2017	2	1
Sandie Dawe CBE to 14 August 2017	2	2
Jim Dixon to 31 July 2017	2	0
David Michael non-executive member from 1 June 2017	3	3
Carole Murray non-executive member from 1 June 2017	3	3

Finance, Staffing and Resources Committee
The Committee met on three occasions during the year and was quorate at each meeting. It is chaired by a trustee. The Committee also met on a fourth occasion sitting as the Remuneration Committee to agree performance bonuses for senior staff.

The Chief Executive attended each Committee meeting as a member. The Director of Finance and

Corporate Services, and Director of Operations attend meetings, and other senior staff attend as required. The Committee is supported and serviced by the Secretariat.

The Committee has oversight on staffing and recruitment controls exercised by senior managers. The Committee also reviewed and approved during the year:

- management accounts and financial management information (including efficiency targets);
- performance data against operational and service standards;
- other performance management data;
- staffing levels and personnel data such as sickness absence, training and development spending;
- IT investment propositions; and
- functional strategies for IT, Estates, HR and Finance.

The Committee approved the proposed budgets for grant programmes and administration for submission to the Board. The Committee also recommended the 2018–19 Business Plan.

The Committee meeting minutes are shared with the Board, as is a formal six-monthly report on business. The Committee Chair orally updates the Board on Committee business and decisions. In 2017–18 the trustees decided to appoint a non-executive independent member to supplement the trustees on the committee. As a result, Steve Blake joined the Committee in 2017. He has considerable experience of financial management, business planning and change management. The Terms of Reference of the Committee were updated to reflect the new role.

Attendance at committee meetings throughout 2017–18 was as follows:

Trustee	Eligible meetings	Meetings attended
Atul Patel MBE Chair	3	3
Steve Blake non-executive member from 1 June 2017	2	1
Perdita Hunt DL, OBE	3	3
Ros Kerslake OBE	3	3
Sir Peter Luff	3	3

Delegated grant decision making
In 2017–18 the Board delegated some decision making for HLF grants to a subset of trustees acting as Board panels. These covered decisions for the following grant programmes:

- Kick the Dust;
- Skills for the Future; and
- Parks for People (in England this was a joint panel with the Big Lottery Fund).

The trustees have delegated their grant decision making responsibilities for certain types and values of HLF awards to country and regional committees. There are 12 of these committees and each contains a Trustee. In addition to making grant decisions, these committees provide advice to the Board on priorities within their area and act as advocates for the organisation's work as a National Lottery distribution body. Chairs of country and regional committees meet with the Board Chair and the Chief Executive, along with senior staff, twice a year.

New members of these committees have a formal induction with the Chief Executive and senior staff throughout the year depending on the recruitment and appointment cycle. In 2017–18 we undertook formal induction sessions for several new members.

Trustees have also delegated grant decision-making for grants under £100,000 to staff, specifically Heads of Operations in countries and regions. An annual report on the impact of delegated grants across all committees is presented to the Board. All decisions made by committees and staff are reported to the Board.

Tailored Review
As identified in the last Governance Statement, 2017–18 saw DCMS undertake our Tailored Review and this reported in November 2017. The review was a positive endorsement of our work and its breadth, and shows that NHMF is a highly regarded organisation that has transformed communities and heritage across the UK.

Tailored Reviews take place for all non-departmental public bodies every few years and DCMS consulted with our stakeholders to find out their views about how we are working. DCMS concluded that we perform well as an organisation, with 79% of survey respondents seeing us as a 'very' or 'extremely' effective funding body. Our staff are highly regarded as open, helpful and valuable sources of support, and our role as a UK-wide funder with a sole focus on heritage is highly valued.

The review notes that HLF is operating within the context of reducing National Lottery receipts and local authority funding. As a result, it recommended that HLF should become more strategic, effective and efficient to ensure National Lottery funding continues to support the resilience of the heritage sector, benefits people and preserves heritage for future generations.

The review made a series of recommendations for how we can further strengthen our effectiveness and performance. These include clarifying our priorities in our upcoming Strategic Funding Framework and strengthening our strategic partnerships with other funders, experts and governments across the UK.

Report of the trustees and accounting officer

The short and medium term recommendations are already being implemented, including strengthening communications, data management, research and evaluation. Longer term recommendations will await our new Strategic Funding Framework in 2019.

We published an implementation plan to track and deliver the recommendations. We will continue to work with DCMS and other partners, to ensure maximum value for National Lottery players and the best possible support for the heritage sector.

National Lottery income
In 2017–18, alongside all other Lottery distributors, we were presented with projections and analysis of National Lottery income for the next few years. We have continued to work with the Gambling Commission, DCMS and Camelot (the National Lottery operator) to understand the data behind these projections and to assess the risks and opportunities from this work.

Camelot undertook a strategic review of their plans and operations in autumn 2017 and we continue to work with them and other partners on the practical implementation of their plans where this overlaps in our area, for example, in the promotion of The One National Lottery initiative.

We welcome the National Audit Office Report (published December 2017) on National Lottery Funding for Good Causes and endorse its findings. We will continue to work to seek improvements in information and projections for income.

In the light of the decline in income the Board made decisions in December 2017 to ensure effective alignment of income to commitments and reserves. We will continue to carefully and closely monitor this risk throughout 2018–19.

Executive and Senior Leadership Team
The Board delegates day-to-day management to the Chief Executive. Previously, the Chief Executive was supported by a Heads of Department Group and a Management Board consisting of all Directors and Deputy Directors. In 2017–18 the roles of these groups was further defined and clarified to improve governance and decision making. The Heads of Department group has been renamed as the Executive Team and the Management Board has been renamed as the Senior Leadership Team. At the same time, the Managers' Forum, comprising all Grade C managers and above, was renamed as the Leadership Team, reflecting the important role of this group.

The Executive (the Chief Executive and the directors) are now responsible for wider strategic management issues and they also act as the Programme Board for the Business Transformation Programme (see page 39). The Executive meets twice a month.

The Senior Leadership Team (the Chief Executive, directors and deputy directors) are now responsible for the day to day operations of the Fund as well as preparations for our next Strategic Funding Framework. The Senior Leadership Team meets weekly.

Each departmental director provides a monthly report to the Board on activities and issues within their remit. The Chief Executive also holds regular meetings with the Leadership Team consisting of senior and middle managers and ensures Board decisions and directions are communicated directly to key staff. These meetings include verbal reports on activities across all departments as well as discussion of thematic issues affecting all teams e.g. risk management and business planning. The Leadership Team have also been involved in helping the senior leaders develop our new Corporate Strategy – see below.

Structure
The Chief Executive operates a four-department structure of:

- Operations;
- Strategy and Business Development;
- Communications and;
- Finance and Corporate Services.

The Secretariat team reports directly into the Chief Executive.

The annual operating plan – the Business Plan – is developed each year alongside financial budgets and grant programme planning. Like previous years, this year we also closely integrated risk management into the business planning process. The Business Plan is discussed with our sponsor department DCMS. DCMS also sets policy directions and financial directions with which we have complied in our National Lottery activities. The Scottish and Welsh governments have also issued some policy directions with regard to National Lottery activities in those countries and we have also complied with those.

We operate in line with a Management Agreement and Financial Memorandum between ourselves and DCMS. This is supplemented by regular meetings with DCMS officials and other National Lottery distributors. The Management Agreement was refreshed last year and a new agreement was put in place for 2016 to 2020. There were no substantive changes to this to report.

Corporate Strategy
We recognised that in addition to the successful strategic plans and frameworks we have, historically, had in place for National Lottery grant giving; we also needed a wider, organisational Corporate Strategy for the direction of the organisation and to

help us plan and respond to future challenges, risks and opportunities.

The Corporate Strategy provides for an 'overarching umbrella' for our activity at a high level. It will be supported by a range of other corporate responses, which provide more detail in specific operational, strategic and policy areas, including our:

- Strategic Funding Framework for National Lottery income 2019 to 2024;
- Business Plan for 2018–2019 for HLF and NHMF;
- Tailored Review Implementation Plan;
- Business Transformation Programme; and
- Business strategies for individual functional areas, e.g. our Digital Strategy.

The National Lottery will remain our most significant source of income from 2018 to 2021, and the focus of most of our activity. Demand for our funding is growing as other public sources of funding decline, with demand outstripping our budget five times over at some levels, against forecasts of reduced National Lottery revenues in future.

The Corporate Strategy reinforces the direction we've been taking for several years, setting out our role as the largest source of funding for heritage across the UK, and taking further steps towards a stronger leadership position, with a particular focus on the opportunities beyond pure grant giving. The goal is to drive change and increase our impact across the UK's heritage, by strengthening our leadership role and standing up for the benefits that heritage can deliver to society.

We will work through due diligence and viability processes to explore the options to expand NHMF's activities in support of the sectors it works with.

Business Transformation Programme
Like all organisations, we recognise we need to adapt and change how we work to the changing environment that we work within. In addition, to deliver our Corporate Strategy we will need to change the way we work.

There have been some changes that impact on the external environment we work within. For example, the referendum to leave the European Union, the continuing devolutionary arrangements across the UK, the impacts of austerity and reduced public sector spending. We are assessing these impacts on our existing and future investments and have addressed other business areas as well as our core business within our Corporate Strategy.

The Tailored Review recognised our achievements over the last two decades, as well as recognising the need for us to adapt and change to respond to this different environment and provide even better

value for money for National Lottery players and the communities and sectors we serve.

We have therefore set up a business transformation programme to change the way we work and how we carry out that work. 2017–18 saw preliminary planning and preparation for this work and 2018–19 will see the first year of delivery and implementation. We expect this to take place over three years before it is fully completed.

To make HLF 'fit for the future', the programme's goals are to deliver:

- the new three-year Corporate Strategy starting in March 2018;
- a simpler, more customer-focused National Lottery funding framework in 2019;
- a radically improved grant management process and system in 2020;
- IT modernisation that supports operational efficiency and customer satisfaction;
- the corporate infrastructure (skills, structure, support services) to support our strategic direction; and
- more agile ways of working and a stronger, more positive culture.

The programme will have seven work streams covering:

- delivery of the new Corporate Strategy;
- the new Strategic Funding Framework;
- review of business processes;
- governance;
- IT modernisation;
- people and estates; and
- marketing/communications and customer insight.

In 2018–19 we plan to:

- Start a phased implementation of the new Corporate Strategy looking especially at diversifying income sources and leveraging greater investment into the heritage sector.
- Deliver all the arrangements for the new Strategic Funding Framework including public consultation, portfolio design, new process and guidance.
- Changes to our website, online portal, forms and processes.
- Start implementation of our digital strategy including completing mobilisation of IT for all staff, Office 365 roll out, integrate telephony, reduce paper, develop a proof of concept approach for a potential new grant management system and portal.

- Review our organisational design/estates footprint.
- Identify ways to improve our external communications, marketing and understand our customers better in a way that improves their experience and interactions with us.

Risk management and internal control

Our system of risk management and internal control is designed to manage risk to an acceptable level rather than eliminate risk to policies, aims and objectives. It can therefore only provide reasonable and not absolute assurance. In particular, I am clear that risk management should not stifle innovation or business change where this is needed. The system of internal control is based on an on-going process designed to identify and prioritise the risks to the achievement of policies, aims and objectives and to evaluate the likelihood of those risks being realised and the impact if that realisation occurred.

All policy setting and grant decision making is informed by the risk management culture and approach of the NHMF. A few years ago we overhauled our risk management approach as part of a wider exercise on assurance across NHMF. We have continued to operate this approach in 2017–18.

The risk registers and underpinning process assign a risk owner who is accountable to the Chief Executive for the effective management of that risk. The registers also identify associated risks so that any 'multiplier effect' is taken account of. It also distinguishes between the 'inherent' level of risk (impact and probability) and the 'residual' level of risk so that it is possible to judge the effectiveness of existing controls and mechanism for mitigating the risk. That also permits the risk owner to identify further measures needed to bring the risk within the appetite and the specific dates for those actions.

The Board also reviewed its Risk Appetite for 2018–19 and continued to reflect greater appetite for business change and transformation. The Board also recognised the risks and challenges facing NHMF in 2018–19 especially in its National Lottery distribution role – these are expected to evolve from the principal risks for 2017–18 as set out below. Effective risk management in the year ahead will be particularly important.

We also recognise that well thought through risk taking and innovation to achieve NHMF objectives should be encouraged. I believe that the Fund demonstrates innovation in its choice of grant awards and does not simply resort to making risk-free decisions. In a time of reducing National Lottery funds this will be even more important to ensure that HLF's funding reaches as widely into the community as possible.

To this end we are prepared to accept that some of the organisations that we give grants to will not subsequently demonstrate full competence in the administration of that grant. We learn our lessons, improve our processes and in rare circumstances write off the grant. In cases where we suspect fraud or improper behaviour we will report the case to the police for further investigation. I approve all write-offs and this allows me to monitor the amount each year to provide assurance on our assessment and monitoring procedures.

As can be seen from the relevant note to the accounts, the level of grant write-off is extremely small relative to the level of grants that we distribute each year. On the other hand, the high level of customer satisfaction demonstrated in independent surveys suggests that our working practices are not too onerous on applicants. Consequently, I am able to conclude that there is no cause for concern about the level of risk implicit in our grant giving processes.

In 2017–18, NHMF considered the following to be the most significant areas of risk:

- HLF income decline;
- Strategic Funding Framework is not successfully implemented;
- Tailored Review recommendations are not successfully implemented;
- adverse reaction to change and business transformation; and
- diversification as outlined in the Corporate Strategy is not successful.

Each of these risks has a risk owner at the Executive level charged with managing the risk and ensuring appropriate mitigation actions are undertaken.

Approach to fraud and information risk

NHMF has a fraud policy that is reviewed on an annual basis. All staff in NHMF undertook bespoke Fraud Awareness Training within the last two years, delivered by a specialist assurance team from Moore Stephens supported by the NHMF Finance Team.

This focused on fraud risk in:

- grant giving;
- procurements; and
- general fraud areas.

The training also identified fraud risk areas for NHMF, how those might be identified and combatted to reduce the risk of fraud. We reinforced this with online training in 2016–17. In 2018–19 we will look at new training and awareness opportunities as part of our response to the Tailored Review.

Over recent years we improved risk awareness and intelligence gathering arrangements with other National Lottery distributors and we continued this last year with better sharing of information, combined resources and consideration of the use of specialist third parties to identify fraud risk. We continue to report all potential cases of fraud to the police and actively contact them in such cases to ensure effective investigation.

The Fund has an established whistle-blowing policy (which we have updated recently) which is brought to the attention of staff regularly and available on the Fund's Intranet. The policy is reviewed annually and staff reminded regularly of its existence and application. There were no reported incidents during the year.

NHMF also has an information risk policy, which is compliant with Cabinet Office guidance and the Security Policy Framework. All new staff receive guidance in information security, data protection and Freedom of Information as part their induction. We have undertaken planning and preparations for the new General Data Protection Regulation provisions introduced in May 2018. We also comply with the government guidance on transparency of spend, contracts etc. In 2017–18 we continued to improve procurement controls and processes.

Business critical models
I consider we are compliant with the recommendations contained within the Macpherson Report. I judge that we utilise one business critical model – the cash flow forecast used for setting annual grant budgets out of our National Lottery income. We aim to ensure that we award the highest amount possible in terms of the level of grants without the risk of running out of cash or over extending ourselves.

The model was created around 10 years ago and remains largely in its original form other than extending its lifecycle. The model has been employed against scenarios of different levels of Lottery income, one-off contributions to the Olympics, and significant new grant programmes. We have found that it provides a reasonable forecast of our financial sustainability.

In 2014–15, based on the model, the Board created a Financial Framework setting out grant ratios linked to the total level of commitments, approved actual liabilities, income from the National Lottery and our balance at the National Lottery Distribution Fund (NLDF). We therefore believe that the model and the Financial Framework provide a robust basis for our grant giving. We have continued to use this approach in 2017–18 and used this in modelling for our Lottery income planning scenarios and assumptions.

Board performance and effectiveness
The most significant activity for the Board has been oversight of the continuing roll out of Strategic

Framework 2013–2018 the implementation and grant giving for those new programmes in 2017–18, such as Skills for the Future and Kick the Dust. In addition, the Board has continued to have oversight for the consultation, planning and preparations for the new Strategic Funding Framework commencing in 2019.

The Board membership changed in 2017–18 – although not as much as in the previous year – this has meant a reduction in the degree of churn amongst the trustees.

The Board undertook an interim review of its skills in 2016–17 through a self-assessment model. A full review will follow next year. The Board are satisfied that they continue to meet the requirements of the 2017 HMT Corporate Governance in Central Government Departments: Code of Good Practice. The main findings of that review were to look at improving the balance of skills and competencies across the trustees. We appointed two new trustees (see list of Board members on page 33 in March 2018 and Maria Adebowale-Schwartz and Sarah Flannigan joined us in May 2018.

All newly appointed trustees receive induction at the time of their appointment, which sets out their obligations and duties as a trustee, the work of NHMF and its systems/processes thereby helping them make a full contribution to the workings of the Board. This formal induction programme is continued through the on-going programme of events and other training opportunities for trustees. The effectiveness of trustees is appraised by the Chair on a regular basis. The Chair's performance is also overseen by the Senior Independent Trustee (the Chair of the Audit and Risk Committee).

Nothing of concern emerged from any of the Committees supporting the Board. Report findings from both the internal and external auditors were satisfactory during the year. There were no matters from the auditors put to the Audit and Risk Committee on behalf of the Board that gave it cause for any concern. The Board therefore believes that it can rely on the information and assurance provided by management for its decision making.

The governance year
As Accounting Officer I have responsibility for reviewing the effectiveness of the systems of internal control. My review is informed by the work of the internal auditors (Moore Stephens) and senior management within the NHMF who have responsibility for ensuring the effective maintenance and implementation of the internal control framework alongside comments made by the external auditors in their management letter and other reports.

All senior staff have performance agreements set at the beginning of the year articulating their personal and corporate objectives for the year. These are linked to the Business Plan and our strategy. These are reviewed formally at mid-year and end-year reviews. I also hold informal meetings with directors on a one-to-one basis throughout the year. As mentioned, the Executive and Senior Leadership teams meet regularly.

I have seen the Management Letter prepared by the external auditors following their audit of the financial statements for the year ended 31 March 2018.

As a result of their programme of work the internal auditors have produced an opinion and annual certificate of assurance with regard to the adequacy of the systems and the operation of internal controls within NHMF. This opinion certifies that there is an adequate and effective system of governance, risk management and internal controls to address the risk that management's objectives are not fully achieved.

The internal auditors upon appointment produced a three-year audit strategy. Last year, this covered the third year of this period and all intended reviews were undertaken and completed on time. The annual plan is extracted from this audit strategy and linked into the risk register and risk appetite. With Moore Stephens we introduced new quarterly liaison meetings with the internal auditors to help monitor progress against plan and redirect resources to emerging risks. These have continued to be used to monitor progress and delivery of the programme.

We also introduced new controls in 2014–15 to improve accountabilities on audit reviews and the implementation of internal audit recommendations. These have continued in 2017–18 and recommendations that were due to be implemented in 2017–18 have been implemented satisfactorily. Three recommendations have been deferred to 2018–19 with the agreement of the Audit and Risk Committee.

All reports of the internal auditors are discussed by the Audit and Risk Committee with senior members of staff in attendance, including those whose departments were reported upon – this gives the Committee and me the opportunity to discuss in detail the findings, recommendations and proposed management actions. Where recommendations for improvements or correction were accepted directors also had to provide an implementation response and timetable for each recommendation. The implementation of these recommendations are tracked and monitored by the Finance and Corporate Services Department and the internal auditors. That control list is also seen as a standing item by the Audit and Risk Committee.

I also require all senior and middle managers to sign annual memoranda of representation to me,

detailing their responsibilities and confirming they have carried out these responsibilities in 2017–18. All managers have signed the memorandum and they are aware that I have placed reliance on those assertions in this statement.

From April 2015, Letters of Delegated Authorities for all Directors were introduced – setting out their delegated authorities (financial, procurement etc.) to be agreed at the start of the year to complement the memorandum at the year end. This cycle has been completed in 2017–18.

As a result of the above, I believe that the Fund's control framework provides me with the level of assurance that I require. There is nothing of which I am aware that leads me to believe that our processes for detecting and responding to inefficiency, for preventing conflicts of interest, for preventing and detecting fraud and for minimising losses of grant in aid and Lottery grants are not adequate.

Ros Kerslake OBE
Chief Executive and Accounting Officer
29 June 2018

Remuneration and staff report

Remuneration of the Chair and trustees
All trustees were entitled to receive an annual salary for time spent on the activities of NHMF.

In addition NHMF reimbursed travel expenses of certain trustees when travelling from their homes to their office of employment in London, Edinburgh, Cardiff or Belfast. NHMF also provided trustees and members of regional and country committees with meals when they were holding meetings at their places of employment. The Fund met the tax liability on all of these expenses. Sir Roger De Haan CBE waived his right to receive a salary in 2016–17.

The remuneration of trustees, including reimbursement of taxable expenses and the tax thereon, falls into the bands in the table on the right. All trustees are appointed by the Prime Minister. They have three-year appointments, which are potentially renewable for a second term. They are not members of the pension schemes used by NHMF. No contributions were made by the Fund to a pension scheme on the trustees' behalf.

Trustees' remuneration was allocated between NHMF and its Lottery distribution activities on the basis of 1%:99%. The total remuneration of trustees in 2017–18 was £191,969 (2016–17: £203,228). The pay and contracts of trustees are discussed and set by DCMS. Their contracts do not contain any

Remuneration of the Chair and trustees (audited information)

	2017–18 £'000	2016–17 £'000
Sir Peter Luff Chair	40–45	40–45
Baroness Kay Andrews OBE	20–25	20–25
Anna Carragher	20–25	10–15
Sir Neil Cossons OBE	10–15	10–15
Sandie Dawe CBE to 14 August 2017	0–5	5–10
Dr Angela Dean	5–10	5–10
Sir Roger De Haan CBE to 19 January 2017	n/a	0–5
Jim Dixon	5–10	10–15
Dr Claire Feehily from 1 March 2018	0–5	n/a
David Heathcoat-Amory to 19 January 2017	n/a	5–10
Perdita Hunt DL, OBE	5–10	5–10
Steve Miller	5–10	10–15
Richard Morris OBE	5–10	10–15
René Olivieri from 1 March 2018	0–5	n/a
Atul Patel MBE	10–15	15–20
Dame Seona Reid DBE	20–25	20–25
Dr Tom Tew	10–15	10–15

bonus clauses. There were no benefits in kind or non-cash elements paid to trustees or directors.

Bonuses payable to senior management are disclosed separately. This is in line with Employer Pensions Notice 359 issued by the Cabinet Office in April 2013.

Cash equivalent transfer values (CETV)
CETV is the actuarially assessed capitalised value of the pension scheme benefits accrued by a member at a particular point in time. The benefits valued are the member's accrued benefits and any contingent spouse's pension payable from the scheme. A CETV is a payment made by a pension scheme or arrangement to secure pension benefits in another pension scheme or arrangement when the member leaves a scheme and chooses to transfer the benefits accrued in their former scheme. The pension figures shown relate to the benefits that the individual has accrued as a consequence of their total membership of the pension scheme, not just their service in a senior capacity to which disclosure applies.

The figures include the value of any pension benefit in another scheme or arrangement that the member has transferred to the civil service pension arrangements. They also include any additional pension benefit accrued to the member as a result of their buying additional pension benefits at their own cost. CETVs are worked out in accordance with the Occupational Pension Schemes (Transfer

Values) (Amendment) Regulations 2008 and do not take account of any actual or potential reduction to benefits resulting from lifetime allowance tax that may be due when pension benefits are taken.

Real increase in CETV
This reflects the increase in CETV that is funded by the employer. It does not include the increase in accrued pension due to inflation, contributions paid by the employee (including the value of any benefits transferred from another pension scheme or arrangement) and uses common market valuation factors for the start and end of the period.

With the exception of Helen Coley-Smith, all senior employees had permanent contracts of employment. All senior employees were ordinary members of the Principal Civil Service Pension Scheme (PCSPS) or alpha. Their costs were allocated between HLF and NHMF on the basis of 99%:1% (2016–17 – 99%:1%). The Director of Business Transformation, Helen Coley-Smith, was appointed to a Fixed Term Contract in 2017, which was reflective of the time bound nature of her role.

The remuneration of senior managers is performance-related, assessed against individual objectives and overall contribution to corporate goals. Performance and remuneration is reviewed annually by the Finance, Staffing and Resources Committee and rated on a scale of four levels of achievement.

Remuneration ratio (audited information)
One of the outcomes of the Hutton Review of Fair Pay is that we are required to disclose the relationship between the remuneration of the highest paid director and the median remuneration of our workforce.

The annualised banded remuneration of the highest paid director in both 2017–18 and 2016–17 was £140,000 to £145,000 including bonus. This was about 5.0 times (2016–17: 5.2 times) the median remuneration of the workforce, which was £28,537 (2016–17: £27,100). There were no employees who received remuneration in excess of the highest paid director. Remuneration ranged from £15,000 to £140,000 (2016–17 £15,000 to £140,000). The highest paid director was subject to the government's pay remit. This restricted the sum available to fund staff pay rises to 1% of the payroll.

Exit packages (audited information)
Under the terms of Employer Pensions Notice 296, issued by the Cabinet Office in March 2011, NHMF is required to publish details of all exit packages agreed in the financial year under review. Falling under the definition of exit packages are compulsory and voluntary redundancies, early retirement, compensation for loss of office, ex-gratia payments etc.

Report of the trustees and accounting officer

Remuneration of employees (audited information)

The remuneration of directors is set out in the two tables below:

	Salary 2017–18 £'000	Salary 2016–17 £'000	Bonus 2017–18 £'000	Bonus 2016–17 £'000	Pension benefits accrued during 2017–18 £'000	Pension benefits accrued during 2016–17 £'000	Total 2017–18 £'000	Total 2016–17 £'000
Ros Kerslake OBE Chief Executive and Accounting Officer from 4 July 2016	135–140	100–105*	5–10	0–5	53	39	195–200	140–145
Eilish McGuinness Director of Operations	80–85	80–85	5–10	0–5	9	18	95–100	105–110
Judith Cligman Director of Strategy and Business Development	95–100	95–100	0–5	0–5	4	21	105–110	120–125
Colin Bailey Director of Finance and Corporate Services	100–105	100–105	5–10	5–10	31	30	135–140	140–145
Louise Lane Director of Communications	80–85	80–85	0–5	0–5	6	60	90–95	145–150
Helen Coley-Smith Director of Business Transformation from 20 April 2017	100–105*	n/a	0–5	n/a	41	n/a	145–150	n/a

	Real increase in pension and lump sum £'000	Total accrued pension at age 60 and lump sum £'000	Cash Equivalent Transfer Value (CETV) at 31/03/18 £'000	CETV at 31/03/17[#] £'000	Real increase in CETV funded by NHMF £'000
Ros Kerslake OBE Chief Executive and Accounting Officer from 4 July 2016	2.5–5	5–10	87	36	40
Eilish McGuinness Director of Operations	0–2.5 and 0–2.5 lump sum	20–25 plus 65–70 lump sum	456	419	7
Judith Cligman Director of Strategy and Business Development	0–2.5 and 0–2.5 lump sum	40–45 plus 120–125 lump sum	907	846	4
Colin Bailey Director of Finance and Corporate Services	0–2.5	5–10	113	82	19
Louise Lane Director of Communications	0–2.5 and 0–2.5 lump sum	20–25 plus 60–65 lump sum	484	462	6
Helen Coley-Smith Director of Business Transformation from 20 April 2017	0–2.5	0–5	29	0	21

* The full year equivalent of Ros Kerslake's salary in 2016–17 was in the band £135,000 to £140,000. The full year equivalent of Helen Coley-Smith's salary in 2017–18 was in the band £110,000 to £115,000.

or at date of appointment if later.

Bonuses payable to senior management are disclosed separately on an accrued basis. This is in line with Employer Pensions Notice 359 issued by the Cabinet Office in April 2013.

The accrued pension quoted is the pension the member is entitled to receive when they reach pension age or immediately on ceasing to be an active member of the scheme if they are already at or over pension age. Pension age is 60 for members of classic, premium and classic plus, 65 for members of nuvos and the higher of 65 or state pension age for members of alpha. The pension figures quoted for directors show pension earned in PCSPS or alpha as appropriate. Where the director has benefits in both PCSPS and alpha the figure quoted is the combined value of their benefits in the two schemes, but note that part of that pension may be payable from different ages.

There was one in 2017–18 (2016–17: none) in the following band:

	2017–18 Number	2016–17 Number
£45,001–£50,000	1	0

99% of the cost of this exit package was charged to our National Lottery distribution activities.

Staff costs and numbers (audited information)

	2017–18 £'000	2016–17 £'000
Salaries	127	277
Employer's NI payments	11	14
Payments to pension schemes	25	53
Temporary staff costs	3	2
	166	346

Additional costs of £13,076,000 have been allocated to National Lottery distribution activities and are reflected in those accounts.

The average number of employees during the year was as follows:

	2017–18 Number	2016–17 Number
Grant applications	4	11
Finance and corporate services	0	0
Strategy and business development	0	0
Communications	0	0
	4	11

The above figures are disclosed as full-time equivalents and include an average of one staff on a fixed term contract. Additionally an average of 267 permanent staff and 27 on fixed term contracts were employed on Lottery distribution activities.

Pensions
Pension benefits are provided through civil service pension arrangements. From April 2015 a new pension scheme for civil servants was introduced – the Civil Servants and Others Pension Scheme or alpha, which provides benefits on a career average basis with a normal pension age equal to the member's state pension age (or 65 if higher). From that date all newly appointed civil servants and the majority of those already in service joined alpha. Prior to that date, civil servants participated in PCSPS, which has four sections: three providing benefits on a final salary basis (classic, premium and classic plus) with a normal pension age of 60; and one providing benefits on a whole career basis (nuvos) with a normal pension age of 65.

These statutory arrangements are unfunded with the cost of benefits met by monies voted by parliament each year. Pensions payable under classic, premium, classic plus, nuvos and alpha are increased annually in line with legislation for pension increases. Existing members of PCSPS who were within 10 years of their normal pension age on 1 April 2012 remained in PCSPS after 1 April 2015. Those who were between 10 years from their normal pension age and 13 years and 5 months from their normal pension age on 1 April 2012 will switch into alpha between 1 June 2015 and 1 February 2022. All members who switch to alpha have their PCSPS benefits banked, with those who have earlier benefits in one of the final salary sections of PCSPS having those benefits based on their final salary when they leave alpha. Members who joined from October 2002 may opt for either the appropriate defined benefit arrangement or a money purchase stakeholder pension with an employer contribution (a partnership pension account).

Employee contributions are salary-related and range between 4.6% and 8.05% of pensionable earnings for members of classic, premium, classic plus, nuvos and alpha. Benefits in classic accrue at the rate of 1/80th of final pensionable earnings for each year of service. In addition a lump sum equivalent to three years of initial pension is payable on retirement. For premium, benefits accrue at the rate of 1/60th of final pensionable earnings for each year of service. Unlike classic there is no automatic lump sum. Classic plus is essentially a hybrid with benefits for service before 1 October 2002 calculated broadly as per classic and benefits for service from October 2002 worked out as per premium. In nuvos a member builds up a pension based on their pensionable earnings during their period of scheme membership. At the end of the scheme year (31 March) the member's earned pension account is credited with 2.3% of their pensionable earnings in that scheme year and the accrued pension is uprated in line with pensions increase legislation. Benefits in alpha build up in a similar way to nuvos except that the accrual rate is 2.32%. In all cases members may opt to give up (commute) pension for a lump sum up to the limits set by the Finance Act 2004.

The partnership pension account is a stakeholder pension arrangement. Employer's contributions of £914 (2016–17: £1,791) were paid to two of a panel of appointed stakeholder pension providers. NHMF makes a basic contribution of between 8% and 14.75% (depending on the age of the member) into a stakeholder pension product chosen by the employee from a panel of providers. The employee does not have to contribute, but where they do make contributions the employer will match these up to a limit of 3% of pensionable salary (in addition to the employer's basic contribution). Employers also contribute a further 0.5% of pensionable salary to cover the cost of centrally-provided risk benefit cover (death in service and ill health retirement).

There are currently no members of staff working on NHMF business with a partnership pension account.

Report of the trustees and accounting officer

No member of staff retired early on health grounds during 2017–18.

Further details about Civil Service pension arrangements can be found at the website www.civilservicepensionscheme.org.uk.

Although the schemes are defined benefit schemes, liability for payment of future benefits is a charge to PCSPS or alpha. Departments, agencies and other bodies covered by PCSPS and alpha meet the cost of pension cover provided for the staff they employ by payment of charges calculated on an accruing basis. For 2017–18, employer's contributions of £24,193 (2016–17: £51,262) were paid to PCSPS and alpha at the rates set out as follows:

Salary in 2017–18	% in 2017–18
£23,000 and under	20.0%
£23,001–£45,500	20.9%
£45,501–£77,000	22.1%
£77,001 and above	24.5%

Absence Management
Staff sickness absence in 2017 remained lower than national benchmarks, with overall levels running at 1.3%, slightly lower than 2016 levels of 1.4%. The Fund continues to support and promote wellbeing policies through its provision of an employee assistance scheme and other related benefits including health screening.

Staff Sickness Absence Levels

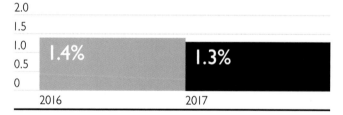

	2016	2017
	1.4%	1.3%

Employee Engagement and Consultation
We continue to regularly consult and inform our staff on our strategic direction and operational progress. This year we have undertaken extensive consultation with staff, customers and stakeholders to help us determine our future Strategic Funding Framework. We have also consulted as part of the development of our new Corporate Strategy.

All staff receive weekly newsletters updating them with news across the Fund and we have active social media discussion groups. We held our first 'town hall' event with all staff in 2018 and now schedule these three times per year. We also regularly convene our Leadership Team, gathering our managers from across our regions and corporate services for discussion and consultation.

The Fund also meets every quarter with its Trade Union partners (FDA and PCS) and meeting minutes are published. Additional meetings are scheduled as necessary and Trade Union views are sought on changes to policy, process and structure.

In 2017, we received the outcomes from our employee engagement survey, which achieved an engagement index figure of 72% (marginally down from last year but still well above comparable benchmarks) based on an 85% response rate.

Equality and Diversity and Employment Monitoring
In all of our activities, we continue to maintain our long-standing commitment to equality and inclusion – in our work-force, in appointing decision-makers and in the reach of our investment. We recognise and appreciate the value of having both a diverse staff group and a diverse Board and committees. We continue to champion equality and inclusion through our organisation, including in our recruitment and selection processes. These goals are explicit in our new Corporate Strategy and our ambition is that our organisation and people better reflect the population of the UK. However, we recognise that currently we do not reflect this in our staff diversity. The tables below show that 75% of our staff are women, 11% are from black, Asian, or minority ethnic groups, 4% have declared disabilities and 2% have declared as Lesbian, Gay, Bisexual or Transgender (LGBT). However, our data also shows high levels of non-disclosure of personal information and we will be taking action to reduce this in 2018 as part of our drive to recognise and celebrate diversity. Over 50% of our staff have attended equality and diversity training, including our Executive team, and undertaking this is compulsory for all new staff. Actions to address workforce diversity also form a key priority under our HR Plan for 2018–19.

The composition for our decision takers including the Board are: 52% female; 12% black, Asian and minority ethnic groups; 5% declared disability and 8% LGBT. Around 50% of decision takers have participated in an equality and diversity workshop and wider discussion at both board and committee level.

We comply with the Equality Act 2010 and our statutory duties under Section 75 of the Northern Ireland Act 1998. We hold the Disability Confident and Investors in People awards.

Expenditure on consultancy
NHMF spent £15,480 on consultants in 2017–18 (2016–17: £0). NHMF has used the definitions of consultancy contained within annex 6.1 of the Cabinet Office controls guidance: version 4.0.

Whistleblowing
The Fund has a clear and accessible Whistleblowing Policy designed to enable staff to raise concerns and to disclose information that the individual

Staff ethnic origin

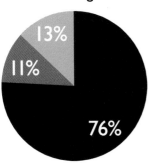

African	7
Asian	1
Asian and White	2
Asian Bangladeshi	1
Asian Indian	4
Asian Pakistani	2
Black African and White	1
Caribbean	5
Chinese	2
Other	7
Other Mixed Ethnic	1
Not declared	39
White	230
Total	**302**

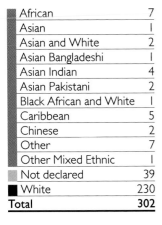

Staff declared disability

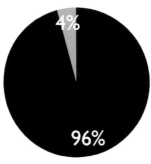

No declared disability	290
Declared disability	12
Total	**302**

Staff sexuality

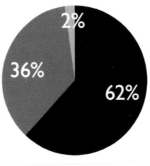

Don't wish to respond	187
Heterosexual	109
LGBT	6
Total	**302**

Data correct at March 2018 and calculated on staff in post headcount (charts contain combined data for staff working on grant-in-aid and Lottery distribution activity).

Staff gender

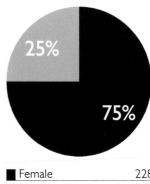

Female	228
Male	74
Total	**302**

believes shows malpractice or impropriety. This covers concerns that are in the public interest and includes the following (non-exclusive) matters:

- financial malpractice or impropriety or fraud
- failure to comply with a legal obligation or statute
- dangers to health and safety or the environment
- criminal activity
- improper conduct or unethical behaviour
- attempts to conceal any of the above.

Tax arrangements of public sector employees

HM Treasury requires all central government bodies to report on the tax status of senior management and long-term contractors. In particular HM Treasury requires all senior managers to be on the payroll and to pay tax under the PAYE scheme. All staff, trustees and regional and country committee members are on the payroll of NHMF and therefore pay tax and national insurance contributions through the PAYE route. We have no contractors that do not meet HM Treasury guidance.

Pension liabilities

The Fund makes contributions to the pension schemes of staff. Other than making these payments the Fund has no pension liabilities.

Ros Kerslake OBE
Chief Executive and Accounting Officer

29 June 2018

Parliamentary accountability and audit report

The certificate and report of the Comptroller and Auditor General to the Houses of Parliament and Scottish Parliament

Opinion on financial statements

I certify that I have audited the financial statements of the National Heritage Memorial Fund for the year ended 31 March 2018 under the National Heritage Act 1980. The financial statements comprise: the Statements of Comprehensive Net Expenditure, Financial Position, Cash Flows, Changes in Taxpayers' Equity; and the related notes, including the significant accounting policies. These financial statements have been prepared under the accounting policies set out within them. I have also audited the information in the Accountability Report that is described in that report as having been audited.

In my opinion:

- the financial statements give a true and fair view of the state of the National Heritage Memorial Fund's activities as at 31 March 2018 and of its operating deficit for the year then ended; and

- the financial statements have been properly prepared in accordance with the National Heritage Act 1980 and Secretary of State directions issued thereunder.

Opinion on regularity

In my opinion, in all material respects the expenditure and income recorded in the financial statements have been applied to the purposes intended by Parliament and the financial transactions recorded in the financial statements conform to the authorities which govern them.

Basis of opinions

I conducted my audit in accordance with International Standards on Auditing (ISAs) (UK) and Practice Note 10 'Audit of Financial Statements of Public Sector Entities in the United Kingdom'. My responsibilities under those standards are further described in the Auditor's responsibilities for the audit of the financial statements section of my certificate. Those standards require me and my staff to comply with the Financial Reporting Council's Revised Ethical Standard 2016. I am independent of the National Heritage Memorial Fund in accordance with the ethical requirements that are relevant to my audit and the financial statements in the UK. My staff and I have fulfilled our other ethical responsibilities in accordance with these requirements. I believe that the audit evidence I have obtained is sufficient and appropriate to provide a basis for my opinion.

Responsibilities of the Trustees and Accounting Officer for the financial statements

As explained more fully in the Statement of Trustees' and Accounting Officer's Responsibilities, the Trustees and Chief Executive as the Accounting Officer are responsible for the preparation of the financial statements and for being satisfied that they give a true and fair view.

Auditor's responsibilities for the audit of the financial statements

My responsibility is to audit, certify and report on the financial statements in accordance with the National Heritage Act 1980.

An audit involves obtaining evidence about the amounts and disclosures in the financial statements sufficient to give reasonable assurance that the financial statements are free from material misstatement, whether caused by fraud or error. Reasonable assurance is a high level of assurance, but is not a guarantee that an audit conducted in accordance with ISAs (UK) will always detect a material misstatement when it exists. Misstatements can arise from fraud or error and are considered material if, individually or in the aggregate, they could reasonably be expected to influence the economic decisions of users taken on the basis of these financial statements.

As part of an audit in accordance with ISAs (UK), I exercise professional judgment and maintain professional scepticism throughout the audit. I also:

- identify and assess the risks of material misstatement of the financial statements, whether due to fraud or error, design and perform audit procedures responsive to those risks, and obtain audit evidence that is sufficient and appropriate to provide a basis for my opinion. The risk of not detecting a material misstatement resulting from fraud is higher than for one resulting from error, as fraud may involve collusion, forgery, intentional omissions, misrepresentations, or the override of internal control.

- obtain an understanding of internal control relevant to the audit in order to design audit procedures that are appropriate in the circumstances, but not for the purpose of expressing an opinion on the effectiveness of the National Heritage Memorial Fund's internal control.

- evaluate the appropriateness of accounting policies used and the reasonableness of accounting estimates and related disclosures made by management.

- conclude on the appropriateness of management's use of the going concern basis of accounting and, based on the audit evidence obtained, whether a material uncertainty exists related to events or conditions that may cast significant doubt on the National Heritage Memorial Fund's ability to continue as a going concern. If I conclude that a material uncertainty exists, I am required to draw attention in my auditor's report to the related disclosures in the financial statements or, if such disclosures are inadequate, to modify my opinion. My conclusions are based on the audit evidence obtained up to the date of my auditor's report. However, future events or conditions may cause the entity to cease to continue as a going concern.

- evaluate the overall presentation, structure and content of the financial statements, including the disclosures, and whether the financial statements represent the underlying transactions and events in a manner that achieves fair presentation.

I communicate with those charged with governance regarding, among other matters, the planned scope and timing of the audit and significant audit findings, including any significant deficiencies in internal control that I identify during my audit.

In addition, I am required to obtain evidence sufficient to give reasonable assurance that the income and expenditure reported in the financial statements have been applied to the purposes intended by Parliament and the financial transactions conform to the authorities which govern them.

Other Information
The Trustees and the Accounting Officer are responsible for the other information. The other information comprises information included in the Annual Report, other than the parts of the Accountability Report described in that report as having been audited, the financial statements and my auditor's report thereon. My opinion on the financial statements does not cover the other information and I do not express any form of assurance conclusion thereon. In connection with my audit of the financial statements, my responsibility is to read the other information and, in doing so, consider whether the other information is materially inconsistent with the financial statements or my knowledge obtained in the audit or otherwise appears to be materially misstated. If, based on the work I have performed, I conclude that there is a material misstatement of this other information, I am required to report that fact. I have nothing to report in this regard.

Opinion on other matters
In my opinion:

- the parts of the Accountability Report to be audited have been properly prepared in accordance with Secretary of State directions made under the National Heritage Act 1980; and

- in the light of the knowledge and understanding of the National Heritage Memorial Fund and its environment obtained in the course of the audit, I have not identified any material misstatements in the Performance Report or the Accountability Report; and

- the information given in the Performance Report and Accountability Report for the financial year for which the financial statements are prepared is consistent with the financial statements.

Matters on which I report by exception
I have nothing to report in respect of the following matters which I report to you if, in my opinion:

- adequate accounting records have not been kept or returns adequate for my audit have not been received from branches not visited by my staff; or

- the financial statements and the parts of the Accountability Report to be audited are not in agreement with the accounting records and returns; or

- I have not received all of the information and explanations I require for my audit; or

- the Governance Statement does not reflect compliance with HM Treasury's guidance.

Report
I have no observations to make on these financial statements.

Sir Amyas CE Morse
Comptroller and Auditor General

6 July 2018

National Audit Office
157–197 Buckingham Palace Road
Victoria
London SW1W 9SP

The financial statements

Statement of comprehensive net expenditure
for the year ended 31 March 2018

	Notes	£'000	2017–18 £'000	Restated 2016–17 £'000
Sundry operating income	4		**233**	0
New standard awards made in the year	13	**(5,735)**		(8,827)
LPOW Roof Repair Fund*				
awards made in the year	13	**(1,236)**		(23,685)
De-committed awards	13	**694**		1,418
Prior year adjustment				
– provision for lapsed commitments	13			924
			(6,277)	(30,170)
Staff costs	22	**(166)**		(346)
Depreciation	9	**(2)**		(2)
Other operating charges	5	**(180)**		(648)
			(348)	(996)
Operating expenditure			**(6,625)**	(31,166)
Operating deficit			**(6,392)**	(31,166)
Profit on the sale of investments	6	**153**		646
Interest receivable	7	**51**		26
Non-operating income			**204**	672
Comprehensive net expenditure				
transferred to the accumulated fund			**(6,188)**	(30,494)
Other comprehensive income				
Net gain on revaluation of				
available for sale financial assets	17		**346**	6,130
Total comprehensive expenditure				
for the year ended 31 March 2018			**(5,842)**	(24,364)

* Listed Places of Worship: Roof Repair Fund

The statement of comprehensive net expenditure excludes the Lottery activities of NHMF, which are reported in a separate set of accounts. All figures shown relate to continuing activities. The notes on pages 54 to 63 form part of these accounts.

Statement of changes in taxpayers' equity
for the year ended 31 March 2018

	Fair value reserve £'000	Income and expenditure account £'000
Balance at 31 March 2016	9,845	18,551
Changes in taxpayers' equity in 2016–17		
Net loss on revaluation of investments	6,130	0
Comprehensive net expenditure transferred to the accumulated fund	0	(30,494)
Grant-in-aid from DCMS	0	35,250
Balance at 31 March 2017	15,975	23,307
Changes in taxpayers' equity in 2017–18		
Net gain on revaluation of investments	346	0
Comprehensive net expenditure transferred to the accumulated fund	0	(6,188)
Grant-in-aid from DCMS	0	12,458
Balance at 31 March 2018	**16,321**	**29,577**

The fair value reserve relates to the difference between book cost and market value of the investments in the endowment fund (see note 10 on page 57). The difference between book and market value of property, plant and equipment (see note 9 on page 57) is not material.

Statement of financial position
as at 31 March 2018

	Notes	31 March 2018 £'000	Restated 31 March 2017 £'000
Non-current assets			
Property, plant and equipment	9	**4**	6
Long-term financial assets available for sale	10	**43,939**	43,856
		43,943	43,862
Current assets			
Trade and other receivables	11	**235**	2
Cash and cash equivalents	8	**7,049**	3,411
Cash held in the endowment fund	10	**0**	0
		7,284	3,413
Total assets		**51,227**	47,275
Current liabilities			
Payables	12	**(69)**	(146)
Grant liabilities due within one year	13	**(5,260)**	(7,847)
Non-current assets plus net current assets		**45,898**	39,282
Non-current liabilities			
Grant liabilities due after one year	13	**0**	0
Assets less liabilities		**45,898**	39,282
Taxpayers' equity			
Fair value reserve	17	**16,321**	15,975
Income and expenditure account		**29,577**	23,307
		45,898	39,282

This statement excludes balances relating to the Lottery distribution activities of NHMF, which are separately disclosed in the accounts of HLF. The notes on pages 54 to 63 form part of these accounts.

Sir Peter Luff
Chair
29 June 2018

Ros Kerslake OBE
Chief Executive and Accounting Officer

Statement of cash flows
for the year ended 31 March 2018

	Notes	2017–18 £'000	2016–17 £'000
Operating activities			
Cash from sundry operating income	4	**233**	0
Cash paid to and on behalf of employees		**(155)**	(326)
Interest received	7	**51**	26
Cash paid to suppliers		**(501)**	(837)
Cash paid to grant recipients	13	**(8,864)**	(36,069)
Net cash outflow from operating activities	15a	**(9,236)**	(37,206)
Investing activities			
Capital expenditure and financial investment	15b	**0**	(2)
Endowment fund net cash receipts	15b	**416**	1,921
Net cash inflow from returns on investments		**416**	1,919
Cash flow before financing		**(8,820)**	(35,287)
Financing activities			
Grant-in-aid received	15c	**12,458**	35,250
Increase/(decrease) in cash and cash equivalents		**3,638**	(37)

The notes on pages 54 to 63 form part of these accounts.

Reconciliation of net cash flow to movement in net funds
for the year ended 31 March 2018

	2017–18 £'000	2016–17 £'000
Increase/(decrease) in operating cash in the period	**3,638**	(37)
Cash used to increase liquid resources	**0**	0
Changes in cash and cash equivalents	**3,638**	(37)
Cash and cash equivalents at 1 April 2017	**3,411**	3,448
Cash and cash equivalents at 31 March 2018	**7,049**	3,411

The notes on pages 54 to 63 form part of these accounts.

Notes to the accounts
for the year ended 31 March 2018

1. Statement of accounting policies

With one exception, there are no standards and interpretations in issue, but not yet adopted, that the Trustees anticipate will have a material effect on the reported income and net assets of NHMF or its Lottery distribution activities. The anticipated impact of IFRS 9 (Financial Instruments) and 15 (Revenue from Contracts With Customers) is expected to be negligible. IFRS 16 (Leases) will have a significant effect, which will be analysed in the accounts for 2018–19 as it does not become effective until 2019–20.

a) Accounting convention

These accounts are drawn up in a form directed by the Secretary of State for Digital, Culture, Media and Sport and approved by HM Treasury. They are prepared under the modified historic cost convention. Without limiting the information given, the accounts meet the accounting and disclosure requirements contained in the Companies Act 2006 and the FREM, so far as those requirements are appropriate, and accounts' direction issued by the Secretary for the Department for Digital, Culture, Media and Sport (DCMS) in October 2002. The accounting treatments contained in the FREM apply International Financial Reporting Standards (IFRS) as adapted or interpreted for the public sector context. The National Lottery accounts' direction issued by the Secretary of State for Digital, Culture, Media and Sport specifically excludes the preparation of consolidated accounts.

Copies of the Lottery distribution and grant-in-aid accounts' directions may be obtained from the Secretary to the Board, National Heritage Memorial Fund, 7 Holbein Place, London SW1W 8NR.

Where the FREM permits a choice, the accounting policy that is judged to be most appropriate to the particular circumstances of NHMF for the purpose of giving a true and fair view has been selected. The particular policies adopted by NHMF are described within this statement. They have been applied consistently in dealing with items that are considered material to the accounts.

b) Government grants

Our grant-in-aid from DCMS is not treated as income. Instead it is treated as financing because it is regarded as a contribution from a controlling party that gives rise to a financial interest. This is done by making an adjustment to the accumulated fund. No allocation is made between grants for revenue and capital purposes. The amount of grant-in-aid recognised in these accounts reflects the amounts actually drawn down from DCMS during the financial year adjusted for amounts we expect to repay.

c) Donations

Donations are treated differently from money received as part of joint grant programmes. A donor is someone that has no involvement in any decision to spend that money. If there is involvement, then it would be treated as a joint grant programme.

Donations are normally charged to the period in which the funds were received. However, where there is a contractual relationship between NHMF and the donor, the donation is charged to the period when the associated activity occurred, irrespective of when the funds were received. Thus the donations from Tourism NI and the Department for Communities have been assigned to 2017–18, despite the funds being received in 2018–19, as the donation agreement was signed in 2017–18 and the associated grant awards were made in 2017–18.

d) Non-current assets

Non-current assets are defined as those items purchased for the long-term use of NHMF and its Lottery distribution activities where the total cost is above £2,000. Depreciation is provided on a straight-line basis on all non-current assets, including those held under finance leases at rates calculated to write off the cost or valuation of each asset over its expected useful life. These lives are as follows:

Short-leasehold property	– the life of the lease
Office equipment	– 4–10 years
Office fittings	– 4–10 years
Grant-assessment and other software	– up to 5 years

No internally-generated costs are capitalised. Depreciation begins in the month after the asset is put into operation.

e) Investments

Non-current financial assets – our investments – are included in the accounts at market value as reported to us by our investment managers. Realised gains and losses are included in the statement of comprehensive net expenditure and are calculated as the difference between sales proceeds and historic cost. Unrealised gains and losses on these investments are reflected in the fair value reserve, which is disclosed in the statement of financial position and the statement of changes in taxpayers equity.

f) Taxation

No provision is made for general taxation as NHMF is statutorily exempt under section 507 of the Income and Corporation Taxes Act of 1988. NHMF is unable to recover Value Added Tax (VAT) charged to it, and the VAT-inclusive cost is included under the relevant expenditure descriptions in these accounts.

g) Pension

The regular cost of providing benefits is charged to the statement of comprehensive net expenditure over the service lives of the members of the scheme on the basis of a constant percentage of pensionable pay. Almost all of our staff are members of PCSPS or alpha (the follow-up scheme to PCSPS) and the percentage of pensionable pay is notified by the Cabinet Office prior to the start of each financial year. See the remuneration and staff report for further details.

h) Leases

The annual rentals on operating leases are charged to the statement of comprehensive net expenditure on a straight-line basis over the term of the lease. Where leases take the substance of finance leases, and are material, they will be treated as finance leases. Items under finance leases are capitalised at their estimated cost excluding any interest charged by the lessor. Interest payments due under the terms of the lease agreement are charged to the statement of comprehensive net expenditure at the date of each payment made under the lease.

i) Grant decisions

Positive decisions by trustees are recognised in the statement of comprehensive net expenditure at the time of award. De-commitments occur when an award or part award is not taken up by a grantee. The time of recognising a de-commitment depends upon agreement between NHMF staff and the grantee. Whilst this is normally straightforward, NHMF is aware of its contractual requirement to pay up to the full grant award and so is prudent in de-committing awards.

j) Allocation of costs and segmental reporting

IFRS 8 requires information to be provided on segmental reporting where this is relevant to the activities of the organisation. Where relevant, senior management would identify separate streams of activity and assign operating costs to them pro rata based upon the level of grant awarded unless there was a significant difference in the manner in which applications were processed; in these cases appropriate alternative methods would be used. NHMF accounts separately for its Lottery distribution activities, which it is required to do under its Lottery accounts' direction. In addition, note 20 on page 63 separates our income and expenditure between our standard NHMF activity and LPOW Roof Repair Fund. The funds available under LPOW Roof Repair Fund are much larger than for our standard grants and we believe their inclusion makes comparison of expenditure with prior years difficult.

NHMF incurs indirect costs that are shared between activities funded by grant-in-aid and activities funded by the National Lottery. NHMF is required to apportion these indirect costs in accordance with the Treasury publication *Managing Public Money*. This cost apportionment seeks to reflect the specific proportion of time and expenses committed to each activity. At the end of the financial year the proportion of joint costs apportioned to our Lottery distribution activities was 99% (2016–17: 99%).

k) Loans

Trustees are entitled to make loans to heritage bodies under the National Heritage Act 1980. Interest rates and repayment terms are at the discretion of Trustees.

l) Apprenticeship levy

The apprenticeship levy was introduced in 2017–18. Whilst the sums we pay are theoretically available to partially fund the cost of courses undertaken by our apprentices, it is currently unlikely that we will be able to utilise these sums fully. Therefore, it is our policy to write-off the levy in the period in which the payment was made unless there is certainty that the sum will be utilised – i.e. the apprentice is in place and the course is booked.

2. Prior year adjustment – impact on results

We have reduced the balance of our grant liabilities at 31 March 2017 through a prior year adjustment as we consider that they were overstated.

The impact on our reported results for 2016–17 is as follows:

	£'000
Operating deficit reported in the accounts of 2016–17	(32,090)
Prior year adjustment	924
Operating deficit after prior year adjustment	31,166
Income and expenditure account balance at 31 March 2017	22,383
Prior year adjustment	924
Income and expenditure account balance after prior year adjustment	23,307

The prior period adjustment has no material impact on the financial statements for 2015–16 so we have not re-presented the 2015–16 comparative balance sheet figures in these accounts.

For further details on the nature of the prior year adjustment – see note 13.

3. Grant-in-aid

	2017–18 £'000	2016–17 £'000
Grant from DCMS	**12,458**	35,250

The large fall in grant-in-aid reflects the impact of LPOW Roof Repair Fund as that programme comes to an end. £7.46million of grant-in-aid (2016–17: £30.3million) was drawn down to fund grant payments and administrative costs for LPOW Roof Repair Fund. We expect to have to return a small proportion of this funding to DCMS in 2018–19 as some of the LPOW Roof Repair Fund projects may not require all their funding. The remaining £5million represented our standard grant-in-aid.

4. Sundry operating income

This comprises:

	2017–18 £'000	2016–17 £'000
Repayments of grant	**0**	0
Donations and bequests	**233**	0
	233	0

Donations represent receipts from the Northern Ireland Tourist Board (trading as Tourism NI) and the Department for Communities (a part of the Northern Ireland Executive) as part of the European Year of Cultural Heritage. This money was designated for certain awards in Northern Ireland made via the Our Heritage programme, which is normally wholly funded by money derived from the National Lottery. The donation was split with £222,500 being towards grants (Tourism NI £100,000 and the Department for Communities £122,500) and £5,000 towards our administration costs (Tourism NI £5,000).

The Trustees wish to thank these two organisations for their contributions and also the estate of the late June Suzanne Cropley who donated £5,000.

5. Operating deficit

The operating deficit is stated after charging the following:

	2017–18 £'000	2016–17 £'000
Auditor's remuneration	**16**	16
Payments under operating leases		
– leasehold premises	**7**	6
– hire of plant and machinery	**0**	0

There were no non-audit fees paid to the external auditors. Additional costs of £8,073,000 have been allocated to NHMF's Lottery distribution accounts. As disclosed in note 1 on page 54, NHMF is required to apportion its costs to its Lottery distribution activities. At the end of the financial year the proportion of joint costs apportioned was 99%.

An analysis of other operating charges, including the above items, is as follows:

	2017–18 £'000	2016–17 £'000
Accommodation	11	11
Postage and telephone	3	3
Office supplies, print and stationery	4	5
Travel, subsistence and hospitality	10	28
Professional fees		
– grant-related	6	6
– non-grant-related	123	189
Communications	15	13
Sundry expenses	4	4
Office equipment	4	63
LPOW Roof Repair Fund overhead allocation	0	326
	180	648

The LPOW Roof Repair Fund overhead allocation represents costs originally charged to our Lottery distribution activities that were regarded as being indirect LPOW Roof Repair Fund costs. Direct LPOW Roof Repair Fund costs (staff working for the LPOW Roof Repair Fund team and external costs incurred running the programme) were charged directly to LPOW Roof Repair Fund. Indirect costs represent a share of senior management and support department time normally allocated to our Lottery distribution activities. There was no overhead allocation in 2017–18 as the programme is coming to a close and the level of activity was much reduced.

6. Profit on the sale of investments

	2017–18 £'000	2016–17 £'000
Long-term financial assets available for sale	153	646

Profits (or losses) are earned on the disposal of investments held in the endowment fund when NHMF requires funds to pay grants or the administration costs of our investment managers. During the year, we raised £400,000 through the sale of some investments in order to cover the excess of awards made over our annual grant-in-aid.

7. Interest received

	2017–18 £'000	2016–17 £'000
Bank interest received		
– Barclays Bank	0	7
– Lloyds Bank	51	11
– Schroder & Co. Limited	0	8
	51	26

During 2016–17, we switched our main banking from Barclays to Lloyds. We also held cash not required in the short-term with our investment managers if and when they had access to better market rates.

8. Cash and cash equivalents

	2017–18 £'000	2016–17 £'000
Instant access		
– Lloyds Bank	**7,049**	3,411
– Schroder & Co. Limited	**0**	0
Seven-day notice		
– Schroder & Co. Limited	**0**	0
	7,049	3,411

Cash is held in Lloyds to support our day-to-day activities. Funds not required for immediate use were placed with our investment managers when they had access to better interest rates than we could source directly. Schroders placed the money on deposit with other financial institutions. When we switched banking from Barclays to Lloyds during 2016–17 we were able to source higher interest rates than available from Schroders hence all our funds were in Lloyds accounts at the year-end.

We continue to review interest rates available in the market for short-term deposits.

9. Property, plant and equipment

	Short-leasehold property 2017–18 £'000	2016–17 £'000	IT and other equipment 2017–18 £'000	2016–17 £'000	Office fittings 2017–18 £'000	2016–17 £'000	Total 2017–18 £'000	2016–17 £'000
Cost at start of year	3	3	20	18	1	1	24	22
Additions	0	0	0	2	0	0	0	2
Disposals	(0)	(0)	(0)	(0)	(0)	(0)	(0)	(0)
At end of year	3	3	20	20	1	1	24	24
Depreciation at start of year	2	2	15	13	1	1	18	16
Charge for the year	0	0	2	2	0	0	2	2
Adjustment on disposal	(0)	(0)	(0)	(0)	(0)	(0)	(0)	(0)
At end of year	2	2	17	15	1	1	20	18
Net book value at start of year	1	1	5	5	(0)	(0)	6	6
At end of year	1	1	3	5	0	0	4	6

Trustees have considered the current cost values of property, plant and equipment. A review of the current cost values at 31 March 2018 revealed no material difference to historic cost values. Therefore no adjustment has been made to reflect current cost values of property, plant and equipment. The value of property, plant and equipment represents a proportionate split of the assets used by both NHMF's grant-in-aid and its Lottery distribution activities. This split is currently 99% Lottery and 1% grant-in-aid.

10. Long-term financial assets available for sale

NHMF was set up in 1980 as successor to the National Land Fund. Trustees believed that, of the initial grant-in-aid that established NHMF, the sum of £10million should be regarded as the residue of the National Land Fund and was to be treated as an endowment fund. They decided to invest it with the aim to maintain its capital value in real terms when compared to the Retail Prices Index. Beyond that, the investment aim is to achieve sufficient growth in real terms to enable NHMF to meet its obligations. To this end, investment in readily marketable financial assets can be made outside the UK. The table on analysis of investments at the year end on page 65 summarises the spread of investments by type and region.

The aim is that the surplus value of the endowment fund, ie the excess over the current value of the initial £10million, can be drawn down to fund NHMF's grant giving. As mentioned elsewhere in this document, Trustees have now tasked the investment managers with generating an annual income that will be added to the grant-in-aid received from DCMS. This will be done by switching a proportion of the endowment fund from capital accumulation units to income generation units within the Charity Multi-Asset Fund, where the endowment fund is currently invested.

On occasions, Trustees have drawn down funds that take the value of the endowment fund below its target value. Trustees do this reluctantly and only when faced with the possibility of losing a significant part of the UK's heritage. In these circumstances, Trustees monitor the shortfall and use future grant-in-aid to replenish the endowment fund if capital growth does not exceed the increase in the Retail Prices Index.

At 31 March 2018, the original £10million investment would be worth £42.1million taking into account indexation. The actual market value was £43.9million including cash held within the endowment.

The endowment fund comprises the following:

	Market value 2017–18 £'000	Book cost 2017–18 £'000
Long-term financial assets	43,939	27,618
Cash	0	0
	43,939	27,618

The proportion of this fund held in cash is disclosed in these accounts as a current asset as part of the cash balances. The endowment fund is invested in the Charity Multi-Asset Fund run by Cazenove Capital, a trading name of Schroders, which invests in a range of 30 unit and investment trusts across many asset types and geographic markets. Units in the Charity Multi-Asset Fund are sold to raise funds for grant payments and administrative expenses. This is the reason that the assets are described as 'available for sale'. Trustees have no plans to liquidate the entire endowment fund.

	2017–18 £'000	2016–17 £'000
Cost and net book value		
At start of year	27,881	29,156
Additions	0	0
Disposals	(263)	(1,275)
At end of year	27,618	27,881
Net book value		
Listed on the London Stock Exchange	0	0
Unlisted investments	27,618	27,881
	27,618	27,881
Cost	27,618	27,881
Market value	43,939	43,856
Unrealised gain	16,321	15,975

There is no liability to taxation on gains realised by NHMF.

An analysis of investments at the year end was:

	2017–18 %	2016–17 %
Bonds	1	2
UK equity	31	35
Europe equity (excluding UK)	4	2
North America equity	7	7
Japan and other Asian equity	6	4
Emerging market equity	6	5
Global equity funds	9	11
Property	10	9
Absolute return/hedge	16	17
Infrastructure	2	3
Cash	5	2
Commodities	3	3
	100	100

Further information about the underlying investments of the endowment fund is elsewhere in this report.

11. Trade and other receivables – all due within one year

	2017–18 £'000	2016–17 £'000
Repayment of grant	0	0
Prepayments and accrued income	235	2
	235	2

No bad debt provision has been created as none of the above items is considered irrecoverable.

The large increase in accrued income relates to donations owed by Tourism NI and the Department of Communities at the year-end.

12. Payables – amounts falling due within one year

	2017–18 £'000	2016–17 £'000
Operating payables	3	40
Other payables including taxation and social security	18	63
Accruals and deferred income	48	43
	69	146

None of the liabilities of NHMF was secured. Of the above amounts for operating and other payables, £3,000 was payable to central government bodies (2016–17: £63,000).

13. Grant liabilities

	2017–18 £'000	2016–17 £'000
At start of year	7,847	13,746
Grants paid in the year	(8,864)	(36,069)
Standard commitments created in the year	5,735	8,827
LPOW Roof Repair Fund commitments created in the year	1,236	23,685
De-committed awards	(694)	(1,418)
Prior year adjustment	–	(924)
At end of year	**5,260**	**7,847**

Prior year adjustment – one of the risks in making awards to historic buildings is that large estimates and contingencies are required in grant applications as the true state of the roof is unknown until work starts. Sometimes these estimates prove to be overstated and not all the funding we have set aside is required. Following discussions with our auditors, we have come to the view that some of our procedures around this are overly prudent with the result being that we continue to recognise as liabilities sums that are never likely to be drawn down by the grantee. Hence, our prior year adjustment for dead commitments.

We have carried out an exercise to try to identify the likely overstated balances and the result is that our reported liabilities at 31 March 2017 have been reduced by just under £1million. The LPOW Roof Repair Fund programme ends in June 2018 and so we will soon know the accuracy of the provision.

The movement on the provision in 2017–18 was:

	£'000
Opening balance at 31 March 2017	0
Prior year adjustment – creation of provision	(924)
Additional provision identified in 2017–18	(54)
Provision released in 2017–18	151
Balance at 31 March 2018	**(827)**

The balance of grant liabilities at the year-end represents amounts due in the following periods:

	2017–18 £'000	2016–17 £'000
In one year	5,260	7,847
In two to five years	0	0
	5,260	7,847

Liabilities at the year-end represent amounts owing by sector, as follows:

	2017–18 £'000	2016–17 £'000
Balances owing to		
– central government	545	757
– local authorities	348	0
– other bodies	4,367	7,090
	5,260	7,847

14. Commitments

Total future minimum operating lease payments incurred by NHMF are as follows:

	2017–18 £'000	2016–17 £'000
Short-leasehold property		
– not later than one year	8	9
– later than one year but not later than five years	34	34
– later than five years	13	21
	55	64

In addition, short leasehold property lease commitments of £6,354,000 (2016–17: £7,570,000) have been allocated to NHMF's Lottery distribution activities and are disclosed in those accounts. NHMF has no capital commitments contracted for or capital commitments approved but not contracted for.

15. Notes to the statement of cash flows

a) Reconciliation of operating deficit to net cash outflow from operating activities:

	2017–18 £'000	2016–17 £'000
Operating deficit	(6,392)	(31,166)
Interest receivable	51	26
Add back non-cash items		
– depreciation	2	2
Decrease in grant commitment reserve	(2,587)	(5,899)
(Increase)/decrease in receivables (excluding capital and investments)	(233)	3
Decrease in non-capital payables	(77)	(172)
Net cash outflow from operating activities	(9,236)	(37,206)

b) Capital expenditure and financial investment

	2017–18 £'000	2016–17 £'000
Payments to acquire		
– property, plant and equipment	(0)	(2)
– intangible fixed assets	(0)	(0)
– long-term financial assets available for sale	(0)	(0)
Receipts from sales of		
– property, plant and equipment	0	0
– long-term financial assets available for sale	416	1,921
	416	1,919

c) Analysis of changes in net funds

	At 1 April 2017 £'000	Operating cash flows £'000	Grant-in-aid £'000	At 31 March 2018 £'000
Cash at bank	3,411	(8,820)	12,458	7,049

16. Related-party transactions

NHMF is a non-departmental public body sponsored by DCMS. DCMS is regarded as a related party. During the year, NHMF (including its Lottery distribution activities) has had various material transactions, other than grant awards, with DCMS itself and with three entities for which DCMS is regarded as the sponsor department – the Big Lottery Fund, Arts Council England and Historic England. Further details of these transactions and balances can be found in the accounts of the Lottery distribution activities of NHMF.

In 2017–18, NHMF signed agreements with a part of the Northern Ireland Executive (the Department for Communities) and a non-departmental public body sponsored by the Northern Ireland Executive (the Northern Ireland Tourist Board trading as Tourism NI). These bodies agreed to contribute £227,500 towards grants and administration costs of some awards we made in Northern Ireland. At the year-end, these bodies owed £227,500.

In May 2011, the Committee on Climate Change signed an underlease for most of the first floor of NHMF's offices, at 7 Holbein Place, London. In August 2016 the area occupied by the Committee for Climate Change was reduced by about a half with a commensurate reduction in rent and contribution to service charges. The Committee for Climate Change is a non-departmental public body, which is jointly-sponsored by the Department for Business, Energy and Industrial Strategy, Department for Environment, Food and Rural Affairs, the Scottish government, the National Assembly for Wales and the Northern Ireland Executive. This underlease is for approximately 13 years and will result in rental payments to NHMF totalling £1.4million. In addition, the Committee for Climate Change will make contributions towards the cost of running Holbein Place of approximately £48,000 per annum at 2017–18 price levels. At 31 March 2018 the Committee for Climate Change owed us £11,000 for service charges, most of which is reflected in our accounts for Lottery distribution activities.

Trustees and panel members are required to maintain a register of interests in heritage bodies, which is updated every year in conjunction with our Secretariat team. At the start of each panel or Board meeting, Trustees and panel members declare any connection with applicants and absent themselves from any part of the meeting where that grant application is discussed. They take no part in the decision as to whether a grant is awarded nor are they involved in any discussion about that project prior to or subsequent to that grant decision. There are also strict rules on the circumstances in which trustees and panel members can accept paid work

from a grantee. Therefore, trustees are satisfied that in no case did individuals have an influence on the decision-making process for those projects with which they have a connection.

Two trustees had a connection with NHMF grants awarded in 2017–18. Details of interests in Lottery grants are set out in the accounts of the Lottery distribution activities of NHMF.

The Brunel Museum
A grant of £235,500: Tunnel Vision (acquisition of Thames Tunnel Brunel drawings).

Neil Cossons declared an interest as he was a patron of The Brunel Museum.

SS Great Britain Trust
A grant of £160,202: Sir Marc Brunel – collection for the Being Brunel Museum and Brunel Institute.

Neil Cossons declared an interest as he was a patron of The Brunel Museum.

Norfolk Museums Service
A grant of £90,900: Anglo-Saxon Aristocrats from 'near Diss'.

Steve Miller declared an interest as he was the Head of Norfolk Museums Service and Norfolk Arts Service.

In addition, one member of the NHMF advisory panel, which advises trustees on the merit of grant-in-aid applications received, had an interest in an award that the Fund made in 2017–18.

Fitzwilliam Museum, University of Cambridge
A grant of £267,607: Saving Queen Victoria.

Tim Knox declared an interest as he was the director of the applicant organisation.

There were no other commercial transactions in which trustees or staff had a material interest or influence. In 2017–18 there will also have been related-party transactions, in the form of grant payments, relating to awards made and disclosed in previous years. As those related-party transactions have been previously disclosed, they are not repeated here.

17. Fair value reserve

	2017–18 £'000	2016–17 £'000
At start of year	15,975	9,845
Movement in the year	346	6,130
At end of year	16,321	15,975

The reserve relates to the difference between book cost and market value of long-term financial assets available for sale (see note 10 on page 57). The difference between book and market value of property, plant and equipment (see note 9 on page 57) is not material.

18. Financial instruments

IFRS 7, *Financial Instruments: Disclosures*, requires disclosure of the role that financial instruments have had during the period in creating or changing the risks an entity faces in undertaking its activities. Financial instruments play a much more limited role in creating or changing risk for NHMF than is typical of the listed companies to which IFRS 7 mainly applies. NHMF does not have powers to borrow but can invest grant-in-aid derived funds. With the exception of the endowment fund, financial assets and liabilities are generated by day-to-day operational activities rather than being held to change the risks facing the organisation.

Liquidity risk
NHMF received £12.458million as grant-in-aid during 2017–18 and has received a further £5million in April 2018. Furthermore, trustees maintain an endowment fund and its underlying investment in Cazenove's Charity Multi-Asset Fund is widely traded. Trustees are able to liquidate assets on a daily basis should the need arise to fund grant payments. Therefore trustees are satisfied that they have sufficient liquid resources, in the form of their cash balances (worth £7million at the date of the statement of financial position) and the endowment fund (worth £43.9million at the date of the statement of financial position), to cover all outstanding grant awards of £5.3million and administrative liabilities of £194,000. The endowment is invested in a fund that is mostly invested in unit trusts, which are readily marketable; the prices are quoted daily in the Financial Times. NHMF monitors its cash balances on a daily basis and keeps in regular contact with grantees to ascertain their likely cash drawdown requirements. Trustees consider that the Fund is not exposed to significant liquidity risks.

Market and interest rate risk
Cash balances were held in a variety of bank accounts, all at variable interest rates. Our accounts with Lloyds, carried an average interest rate of 0.55%. The small rise in base rates in November

2017 improved the average return slightly. These accounts were used to make grant payments and fund our administration. In previous years, we have sometimes taken advantage of holding sums with our investment managers as they may have access to better interest rates than we can source. However, at present, we enjoy attractive rates from Lloyds and so do not take advantage of Schroders' offers. The sharp decline in market interest rates that occurred during 2008–09, as well as the further cut in 2016–17, has had an ongoing impact on returns, but as there is little room for rates to fall further the risk is small. The year-end cash balances were £7million and were held as disclosed in the table on page 57. Other financial assets and NHMF's financial liabilities carried nil rates of interest.

Schroders managed NHMF's endowment under the trading name of Cazenove Capital Management and invested it in a wide range of assets, from marketable shares to cash. At the year end, the market value of the endowment, excluding its cash element, was £43.9million. Returns are dependent upon global stock and commodity markets and performance of companies included within the portfolio. In the year, the return on the endowment was a rise of 1.1%. Trustees kept the performance of investments under review through their Finance, Staffing and Resources Committee and its Investment Panel, which includes three independent members with extensive experience in financial markets.

As the balance of cash and investments within the endowment fund significantly exceeds the current value of existing liabilities and because NHMF has been informed of the level of its grant-in-aid over the next few years, no detailed sensitivity analysis has been carried out. Should the value of its endowment fund significantly decline in the long term, trustees would seek an increase in their grant-in-aid while reducing their future grant award budgets. Should this request be turned down by the Secretary of State for Digital, Culture, Media and Sport, trustees will review their long-term grant award strategy.

	2017–18 £'000	2016–17 £'000
Cash balances		
– sterling at floating interest rates	7,049	3,411
– sterling at a mixture of fixed and floating rates	0	0
– sterling at fixed rates	0	0
	7,049	3,411

Credit risk
NHMF's receivables mostly comprise amounts owed by the Northern Ireland Executive. It is not, therefore, exposed to significant credit risk.

Notes to the accounts
for the year ended 31 March 2018

Foreign currency risks

The endowment fund is invested in Cazenove's Charity Multi-Asset Fund, which is denominated in sterling. The fund invests in a large number of unit trusts and similar products, many of which include investment in assets denominated in other currencies. It is not possible to be precise about the proportion of the investments denominated in foreign currencies, but it is around 31%. The fund mitigates its exposure to foreign exchange risks by investing in a global spread of equities, bonds and commodities and, therefore, currencies. The trustees' Investment Panel monitors the investment of our endowment fund, including the exposure to foreign currencies within the Fund. All other assets of NHMF are denominated in sterling.

Financial assets by category

	2017–18 £'000	2016–17 £'000
Assets per the statement of financial position		
– non-current assets	**43,939**	43,856
– cash and cash equivalents	**7,049**	3,411
– loans and receivables	**235**	2
	51,223	47,269

Financial liabilities by category

	2017–18 £'000	2016–17 £'000
Liabilities per the statement of financial position		
– other financial liabilities		
• grant commitments	**5,260**	7,847*
• operating payables	**3**	40
• other payables	**18**	63
• accruals	**48**	43
	5,329	7,993

* after prior year adjustment of £924,000

Fair values

Set out below is a comparison, by category, of book values and fair values of NHMF's financial assets and liabilities as at 31 March 2018.

Financial assets at 31 March 2018

	Book value £'000	Fair value £'000
Cash[1]	**7,049**	**7,049**
Investments[2]	**27,618**	**43,939**
Receivables[3]	**235**	**235**
	34,902	**51,223**

Financial assets at 31 March 2017

	Book value £'000	Fair value £'000
Cash	3,411	3,411
Investments	27,881	43,856
Receivables	2	2
	31,294	47,269

Financial liabilities at 31 March 2018

	Book value £'000	Fair value £'000
Grant payables[4]	**5,260**	**5,260**
Operating payables[5]	**3**	**3**
Other payables[5]	**18**	**18**
Accruals[5]	**48**	**48**
	5,329	**5,329**

Financial liabilities at 31 March 2017

	Book value £'000	Fair value £'000
Grant payables	7,847*	7,847*
Operating payables	40	40
Other payables	63	63
Accruals	43	43
	7,993	7,993

* after prior year adjustment of £924,000

Basis of fair valuation:

1. The figure here is the value of short-term money market investments and deposits with commercial banks. It is expected that book value equals fair value.

2. Investments are made in readily marketable securities and are valued at mid-market at close of business on the date of the statement of financial position. Where relevant, the closing exchange rate between the base currency and sterling is taken at the date of the statement of financial position. Book value reflects the price actually paid in sterling at the date of completion of the transaction.

3. No provision for bad debt is deemed necessary. None of the debts are long term and so no discounting factor has been applied.

4. No discount factor has been applied.

5. All payables are due within normal contractual terms, usually 14–30 days, and so no difference exists between book value and fair value.

Maturity of financial liabilities

	2017–18 £'000	2016–17 £'00
In less than one year	**5,329**	7,993
In more than one year, but less than two	**0**	0
In two to five years	**0**	0
In more than five years	**0**	0
	5,329	7,993

19. Statement of losses

NHMF made no losses during the year (2016–17: £0).

20. Segmental reporting

Our statement of comprehensive net expenditure for 2017–18 split between our two functions is as follows. We believe that the operation of LPOW Roof Repair Fund distorts our long-term reporting trend and so we have broken down the income and expenditure between our two activities – see note 1j on page 55 for further information.

	Standard £'000	LPOW Roof Repair Fund £'000	Combined £'000
Sundry operating income	233	0	233
Awards made in the year	(5,735)	(1,236)	(6,971)
De-committed awards	384	310	694
Staff costs	(65)	(101)	(166)
Depreciation	(2)	0	(2)
Other operating charges	(132)	(48)	(180)
Operating expenditure	(5,550)	(1,075)	(6,625)
Operating deficit	(5,317)	(1,075)	(6,392)
Profit on sale of investments	153	0	153
Interest receivable	51	0	51
Comprehensive net expenditure transferred to the accumulated fund	(5,113)	(1,075)	(6,188)
Net gain on revaluation of available for sale financial assets	346	0	346
Total comprehensive expenditure for the year to 31 March 2018	**(4,767)**	**(1,075)**	**(5,842)**

Income received from Tourism NI towards our administration costs has been assigned to Standard in the above table although strictly it belongs to neither category.

21. Events after the reporting period

There were no events that occurred after 31 March 2018 up until the date the Accounting Officer signed these accounts that need to be disclosed. The financial statements were authorised for issue on 6 July 2018 by the Trustees and Accounting Officer on the date they were certified by the Comptroller and Auditor General.

22. Staff costs

	2017–18 £'000	2016–17 £'00
Salaries	127	277
Employer's NI payments	11	14
Payments to pension scheme	25	53
Temporary staff costs	3	2
	166	346

Further information about staff costs is in the Remuneration and Staff Report elsewhere in these accounts.

The Trade Union (Facility Time Publication Requirements) Regulations 2017

Under this statutory instrument, we are required to disclose information about trade union facility time and relevant employee expenditure. This information covers both our grant-in-aid and Lottery distribution activities.

Relevant union officials
What was the total number of your employees who were relevant union officials during the relevant period?

	Number of employees
Number of employees who were relevant union officials during the relevant period	26
Full-time equivalent employee number	4

Percentage of time spent on facility time
How many of your employees who were relevant union officials employed during the relevant period spent a) 0%, b) 1%–50%, c) 51%–99% or d) 100% of their working hours on facility time?

Percentage of time	Number of employees
0%	13
1–50%	13
51%–99%	0
100%	0

Percentage of pay bill spent on facility time
Provide the figures requested in the first column of the table below to determine the percentage of your total pay bill spent on paying employees who were relevant union officials for facility time during the relevant period.

Total cost of facility time	£24,313.52
Total pay bill	£12,954,000

Percentage of the total pay bill spent on facility time, calculated as:

Total cost of facility time ÷ Total pay bill × 100	
(£24,313.52 ÷ £12,954,000) × 100 =	0.2%

Paid trade union activities
As a percentage of total paid facility time hours, how many hours were spent by employees who were relevant union officials during the relevant period on paid trade union activities?

Time spent on paid trade union activities as a percentage of total paid facility time hours calculated as:

Total hours spent on paid trade union activities by relevant union officials during the relevant period ÷ Total paid facility time hours × 100	
(1,107 ÷ 7,280) × 100 =	15.2%

Disclosure of investments

The investment of the endowment fund

Trustees regard a £10million lump sum given to the NHMF in 1980 as an endowment to be occasionally used alongside its grant-in-aid to help support the UK's heritage. The endowment fund is invested in order to maximise the return over the long term.

Investment management is outsourced to specialist fund managers following a tendering exercise. NHMF has been using Schroders since 2010 and the entire endowment fund is invested in Schroders' Charity Multi-Asset Fund. The fund is a common investment fund established and approved by the Charity Commission. During 2014–15 Schroders merged with Cazenove Capital Management and now use the latter name for its charity investment management business.

Investment policy is the responsibility of the Investment Panel – a sub-committee of the Board's Finance, Staffing and Resources Committee. The panel comprises two trustees and three independent financial experts who meet with Cazenove twice a year to discuss its performance.

The Board recognises that there can be public interest in disclosure of the investments being made and sets out details of them below. The Charity Multi-Asset Fund invests in a large number of investment trusts and other types of investment, most of which regularly buy and sell assets. The information was correct at 31 March 2018 and will be updated annually.

Cazenove has its own responsible investment policy that it adopts when making investments. It considers environmental, social and governance issues and produces an annual responsible investment report detailing its activities. Cazenove complies with the United Nations' Principles for Responsible Investment. We require Cazenove to notify us if it is considering investing in any organisation that could lead to embarrassment to NHMF.

Source: Cazenove 31 March 2018

* Absolute return funds – unlike traditional asset managers, who try to track and outperform a benchmark (a reference index such as the FTSE100), these managers employ different strategies in order to produce a positive return regardless of the direction and the fluctuations of capital markets. These funds are sometimes referred to as hedge funds.

Charity Multi-Asset Fund – Investment Selection

UK equities	**30.7%**
Charity Equity Fund	7.5%
Equity Income Trust for Charities	3.8%
Old Mutual UK Alpha Fund	5.8%
Majedie UK Equity Fund	5.3%
Troy Trojan Income Fund	4.1%
Aberdeen UK All Share Tracker	4.2%
Global equities	**9.4%**
Schroder QEP Global Core	9.4%
European equities	**3.9%**
Jupiter European Special Situations Fund	2.0%
Schroder European Alpha Income Fund	1.9%
US equities	**6.6%**
Vanguard S&P 500 ETF	6.6%
Asian equities	**3.1%**
Schroder Asian Alpha Plus Fund	3.1%
Japanese equities	**3.2%**
Schroder Tokyo Fund	3.2%
Emerging market equities	**5.8%**
Schroder Global Emerging Markets Fund	5.8%
Equities	**62.7%**
Absolute return*	**16.2%**
Schroder ISF Emerging Market Debt Absolute Return (£)	2.5%
Ruffer Total Return Fund	3.1%
Troy Trojan Fund	3.1%
Henderson UK Absolute Return Fund	2.7%
Majedie Tortoise Fund	2.6%
Pyrford Global Total Return Fund	2.2%
Property	**9.8%**
Property Income Trust for Charities	3.5%
Charities Property Fund	2.3%
Henderson UK Property Fund	2.1%
Ground Rents Income Fund	1.9%
Infrastructure	**2.4%**
3i Infrastructure	0.8%
HICL Infrastructure	0.7%
International Public Partnerships	0.9%
Commodities	**2.7%**
Schroder Commodity Fund (£)	1.1%
Gold ETF (£)	1.6%
Alternatives	**31.1%**
Bonds	**1.3%**
Twenty Four Absolute Return Credit Fund	1.3%
Cash	**4.9%**
Cash	4.9%
Bonds and cash	**6.2%**

Chair, trustees and management

Acknowledgements

Photography
Cover image: Famous Women Dinner Service © Image courtesy of Piano Nobile Gallery, copyright the Estate of Vanessa Bell and DACS

East Cambridgeshire Bronze Age Torc © The Trustees of the British Museum

Saving *Queen Victoria* © Sotheby's

A Game of Bowls © Sotheby's

Two women in a Garden, The Fry Art Gallery www.fryartgallery.org

Anglo-Saxon Aristocrats grave goods © Norfolk Museums and Archaeology Service

Galloway Hoard © The Trustees of National Museums Scotland

Monson Papers © Lincolnshire Archives, Lincolnshire County Council

Owen Jones designs © Victoria and Albert Museum, London

First Day's Vase © The Potteries Museum & Art Gallery, Stoke-on-Trent

Tunnel Vision at The Brunel Museum © The Brunel Museum

Sir Marc Brunel – collection for the Being Brunel Museum and Brunel Institute © SS Great Britain Trust Collection

Leekfrith torcs © Staffordshire County Council

Designed and produced by The Right Stuff, London
Please recycle after use.